ALSO BY STASSI SCHROEDER

Next Level Basic

Off with My Head

You Can't Have it All

THE BASIC B*TCH GUIDE

TO TAKING THE PRESSURE OFF

STASSI SCHROEDER

G

Gallery Books

NEW YORK   LONDON   TORONTO   SYDNEY   NEW DELHI

G

Gallery Books
An Imprint of Simon & Schuster, LLC
1230 Avenue of the Americas
New York, NY 10020

First Gallery Books hardcover edition September 2024

GALLERY BOOKS and colophon are registered trademarks of Simon & Schuster, LLC

Simon & Schuster: Celebrating 100 Years of Publishing in 2024

For information about special discounts for bulk purchases, please contact Simon & Schuster Special Sales at 1-866-506-1949 or business@simonandschuster.com.

The Simon & Schuster Speakers Bureau can bring authors to your live event. For more information or to book an event, contact the Simon & Schuster Speakers Bureau at 1-866-248-3049 or visit our website at www.simonspeakers.com.

Interior design by Jaime Putorti
Illustrations by Hannah M. Brown

Manufactured in the United States of America

10 9 8 7 6 5 4 3 2 1

Library of Congress Cataloging-in-Publication Data has been applied for.

ISBN 978-1-6680-4992-1
ISBN 978-1-6680-4994-5 (ebook)

For Beau, Hartford, and Messer,

You are my reason for everything.

Contents

CONTENTS

You Can't Have it All

High-Key Tired

*Y*es, this book is called *You Can't Have It All*. It's not a typo.

I get that I've probably struck a nerve here. How dare I tell women that we *can't* have it all, after we've worked so hard for so long to *lean in* and be *boss bitches*? Why would I discourage women from striving to be girlbosses at work and at home, balancing career and kids, friends and partners, and staying on top of all the million little chores and unsung duties that go along with it?

Because . . . having it all is freaking hard. I bribe my toddler with ice cream and cake pops so I can maintain my sanity. I do spot spray tans because I don't have time to do my whole body. When I go to the bathroom in my own home, I have an audience, since Hartford follows me and I pull in Messer and his BabyBjörn bouncer because I obviously can't leave a baby unattended. Over

1

the last two years, I've come to realize that having it all and being a girlboss is not the vibe.

I'm writing this book for you, but also for myself, because I need to learn to take the pressure off. I want to be a chill, soft mom/wife/career woman, but that's way easier said than done.

This is not a fully anti-girlboss book. I love an ambitious woman who goes after everything she wants, plus I'm no stranger to hustle culture and girlbossing myself. But I do have a question to ask: after the brutal, stressful, chaotic years we have all collectively experienced since the pandemic, is being a boss bitch with all her shit together really the vibe? I know I'm not the only one who's high-key tired.

I'm tired of feeling like I should be doing more, accomplishing more, exercising more, socializing more, networking more, buying more. And I'm *really* tired of feeling like I have to master all of these things while simultaneously being the perfect mother, wife, friend, daughter, sister—all while living life very publicly, which, yes, I know I chose for myself, but still. It's like we're all expected to operate at 100 percent in everything we do. It's not enough to be nailing it in your career. Your relationship better be flawless, your house aesthetically pleasing, and your kids should be on a two-year wait list for that school all the other moms are talking about. You also better be sweating through Pilates by midmorning and cooking balanced organic meals for your family by sunset. Spend your precious free time pureeing spinach and peas so you can hide vegetables in your child's gourmet homemade mac 'n' cheese. And don't forget to make time for Botox appointments, because heaven forbid someone see a line on your face.

I've always felt the pressure to excel at everything I possibly could, even if that pressure is usually self-inflicted. I am a Jedi when it comes to pushing myself to do/be/achieve more. It's nobody's fault but my own. Basically, I'm the drama. Society puts pressure on women to do and be all the things, but I also do it to myself.

I'm writing this book to put an end to all the drama I bring to my own life—as a mom, as a wife, as someone who wants to be *all the things*. I'm not just writing this for myself, obviously. It's for you too. But I do see this book a little bit like my own personal literary hype track. I mean, not that I would ever put myself in the same realm or universe as the iconic Taylor Swift, but does she listen to her own breakup songs or self-empowerment songs when she needs to pump herself up? Do you think Taylor puts on "Vigilante Shit" the way I do whenever I feel like someone's done me dirty? It's possible!

The idea of "having it all" is essentially the pursuit of balance in your personal and professional life, which in theory sounds great. I mean, who doesn't want balance in their life? I've wrestled with my feelings about this for a while; I even wrote a chapter in my last book about my thoughts on the phrase *having it all*. All that this outdated, annoying-AF phrase does is put extra pressure on us to balance all the parts of our lives perfectly, with a Juvéderm-filled smile on our faces. (No hate for Juvéderm. It looks lovely on many people, but when I tried it, it was more painful than childbirth and I looked like the clown from *It*.) As if we didn't already lie awake at night stressing about our lives, along came this boss bitch culture making a lot of us feel inadequate or behind in life. My For You page on TikTok is flooded with content from women who sure look like they have it all, and oftentimes it makes me pick myself apart. Do men feel this same need to "have it all"? I doubt it. They can walk into a meeting with their hair all tousled and their clothes wrinkled from the night before and everyone is like, "Dude, work hard, play hard!" If a woman did that—and especially a woman with kids—people would say she was having a mental breakdown.

Listen, I'm not saying men never get asked about "having it all," and I certainly don't want to leave out any men who might be reading this book (all four of you), but there is no way my husband is losing sleep over whether he has it all or not. We say it's about balance, but we all know what "having it all" really means: the career, the husband/partner, the children, the perfect home, the exciting social life, the latest wardrobe, a killer bod, and the mental and emotional stability to match (sans the help of Lexapro). Setting aside the very important fact that now every woman has a different definition of what "having it all" means to her, is having it all—whatever the definition—the thing that's most valuable in life? It's impossible to function at 100 percent in everything we do, so why do we keep putting all this pressure on ourselves? I'm in the mood for a little grace. Yep, I'd like to live in a perpetual grace period where I'm not required to have my shit together at all times.

And naps. I miss naps.

We all had a whole lot of time at home during the pandemic lockdowns, when we were forced to look inward and figure out what really matters to us. I realized that time is precious, and I

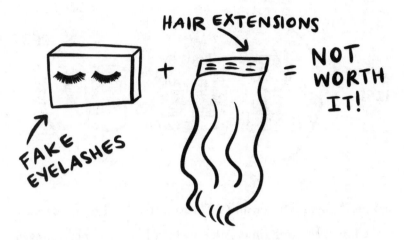

wanted to spend it doing the things that enhanced my freakin' soul. I realized that false eyelashes and hair extensions are actually pretty uncomfy, therefore unnecessary. I realized that after a big ole break from my career, I was still alive and it wasn't the end of the world. The more I've talked to my female friends, the random mom at the park, those of you I've met out and about, and just any woman in general, the more I've realized I am most definitely not alone in my feelings of wanting to pump the brakes. TikTok told me it was time for a vibe check. I checked it. And the constant feeling of having to do more is definitely *not* the vibe.

The irony of this? Before I wrote *Off with My Head*, I was writing an entirely different book, a basic bitch's take on how to be— you guessed it—a girlboss. I still have cringe sweats just thinking about it. But time has passed, and a lot of life has happened. Not only did I age and grow (you know, just standard evolution), but I got married, I became a mom, I was very publicly held accountable for behavior I am not proud of, I was jobless for a while, I

had just bought a home and 2020 required that I never leave that home for a very long time. After a while, I began my career again, which felt like I was reentering the world after having been lost in space for decades. After two and a half years, I felt ready to launch my podcast *Straight Up with Stassi* again. I had done *a lot* of work, soul-searching, and listening. I also had a new perspective about what I wanted out of business, my career, and my life. I wanted to carve a path for myself on my own terms, without higher-ups to dictate what I did or talked about, even if that meant less income. I've realized that I want to be my own boss, to feel free, and to lean into what brings me the most joy. And watching Victorian England ambiance videos on YouTube brings me a hell of a lot of joy.

That's truly what this book is about: learning to accept that fact that it's impossible to "have it all" but knowing you can still have a happy life somewhere in the middle. No, I am not trying to be some life coach who gives you little mantras and tries to sell you bumper stickers with inspirational quotes on them. In this new phase, Stassi 2.0 or 5.0 or whatever, I'm all about taking the pressure off, giving yourself grace, and leaning into what makes you happy, without guilt. I am by no means perfect at this. In fact, I suck at it. I now have two kids, I can leave the house, and I'm working, so I will not lie and pretend that the girlboss ghost of years past doesn't come haunt me now and then. But I'm trying to exorcize the demon.

I once saw a TikTok (shout-out to @ariellelorre) that explained this so perfectly. It said, "The prolonged idea of happiness is actually contentment, which comes from the ability to handle whatever stuff comes our way in life. Master that, and you will be content and will be able to hold on to those moments of joy along the way." This is something I've become rather good at. When life starts to suck, I focus on the things that bring me joy and the things I'm grateful for. That and a bit of self-deprecating humor are my coping mechanisms that keep me sane and happy. To follow that up,

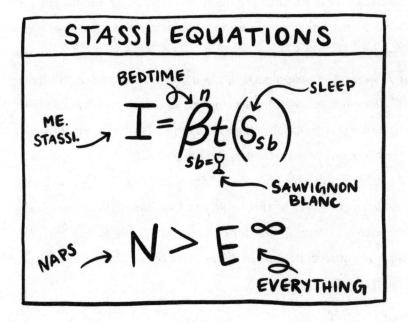

STASSI EQUATIONS

ME. STASSI. → BEDTIME / SLEEP

$$I = \beta t \left(S_{sb} \right)^n$$

$sb = \text{🍷}$ → SAUVIGNON BLANC

NAPS → $N > E^\infty$ → EVERYTHING

ever since I reentered the public space and was able to work again, I noticed that the mood with most people has been shifting, and we've all been thrown into this feeling of just needing . . . peace and joy and appreciation for the things that make us happy. Wow, if season-one Stassi knew that thirty-five-year-old Stassi was going to be preaching about contentment and peace, she would've elected to have someone plunge flaming-hot daggers into her eyes instead of reading this shit. But that's growth! And seriously, all of this pressure to "have it all" is exhausting, and I'm not sure it's the one-way ticket to happiness that we thought it was.

With that said, my real point is this: It's okay to take the pressure off yourself, pump the brakes, chill the *eff* out. It's okay to be unapologetically happy with where you are, to work hard *if you want to*, but to also take a break. "Having it all" to me means appreciating the things and moments that bring me bits of joy: small things like getting a spray tan or finding out that one of my favorite shows is getting renewed, and big things like having the freedom to be unapologetically real and true to myself. It's living life happily even when I have a little less. It's also acknowledging that things will not always go as planned. Not your wedding, not your job, not your birth plan. And that's fine!

There's still a bit of cheugy girlboss energy in me, as you'll read about in the pages of this book, but I've come a long way. And I hope that in reading my stories, you will be able to take the pressure off yourself. Because in the words of queen Kris Jenner, "You're doing amazing, sweetie."

CHAPTER 1

#NotABoss

Apparently, the whole girlboss thing is over. As I'm writing this, it's all about: girl dinner (two pickles, a few olives, three almonds, and a slice of cheese plus wine, for example), hot girl walks (see 2021 TikTok for eight billion examples), and girlie Barbie badass culture. By the time you read this, we will have moved past these things into something else I can't even fathom right now because I just gave birth to a nearly eight-pound human and I'm tired. The point is, as of this moment, the girlboss is dead, or at least seriously out of fashion, but grown adult women embracing their girliness is *everywhere*. Still, I want to talk about the whole girlboss phenomenon and *why* it mattered, and why it then went the way of Juicy Couture velour tracksuits. By the way, if those things make a comeback, I'm giving up on everything. No one, not even my worst enemy, should have to endure that trend twice in one lifetime.

I couldn't tell you the year I first heard about the term *girl-boss*, only that I remember hearing it right around the exact time I actually started feeling like a girlboss. I'm pretty sure the term was coined or at least popularized by the founder of the clothing company Nasty Gal, Sophia Amoruso, since it was the title of her 2015 book *#Girlboss*. The whole idea didn't resonate with me until a couple of years later though. I'm going to be honest: I felt like I was destined for girlboss culture. It was a written-in-the-stars match for me. *Stassi Schroeder* and *girlboss* were one in the same in my eyes, which is seriously embarrassing to admit, since nowadays the term *girlboss* basically describes a type of cheugy millennial who might post photos of herself holding a mug with an inspirational quote on it, wearing a blazer over a loose T-shirt because she's relaxed but she also means business. Her belt definitely had a Gucci logo and she wore skinny jeans and a red lip to add a pop of color. And you KNOW she captioned her photo *Is it wine o'clock yet???* I'm cringing just thinking about it.

I remember exactly when I first started leaning into girlboss energy. It was right after season four of *Vanderpump Rules*. I was starting to make enough money to feel like I was a bad boss bitch. I had gone from splitting five-dollar footlongs at Subway with Katie Maloney to having the ability to buy not one but multiple Chloé Drew bags from Neiman Marcus. I rode so hard for the Chloé Drew bag, it almost became a personality trait.

It wasn't just the bigger *Vanderpump Rules* paychecks that made me feel like girlbossing was my destiny. It was the fact that my podcast *Straight Up with Stassi* was actually bringing in considerable

THE BAG
OF THE
TIMES

money, and it had gotten popular enough for me to get some of my dream guests. I mean, the second I interviewed Rachel Zoe and Emma Roberts on my podcast, my girlboss metamorphosis was complete.

I felt so proud of myself for building something outside of *Vanderpump Rules*. Girlboss was going to be my whole identity. I also think this appealed to me so strongly because I had gone through some extra-shitty relationships in which I felt belittled, demeaned, and gaslit by my boyfriends. I had one specific boyfriend, aka Manbun, who made me feel like a loser for being on reality TV. If you've seen the show or read my previous books you know all about him, but, much like we treat murderers and psychopaths, I still refuse to dignify his existence with a name. Anyway, after years of feeling like my career was lame, becoming a girlboss on my own terms was my post–toxic relationship glow-up. Instead of getting in better shape or "hotter," I girlbossed. Back then, the term was basically used to describe hustle culture for women. It was about female empowerment, signifying a woman who was ambitious and successful in business. She created something from the ground up, and oftentimes was the face of her own brand, like Sara Blakely. She was a take-charge woman who wasn't beholden to anyone. Girlbosses

11

valued independence above all else. You were personally fulfilled only if you were making your own money. A girlboss is her own boss. A girlboss had it all. I mean, all of these things sound great, right?

Maybe in theory . . .

I started to question girlboss energy the second I got canceled in 2020. Before I was canceled, my self-esteem had always been tied to how much I was accomplishing. Again, a major trait of the girlboss: her identity was directly tied to her professional success. The more I was achieving, the better I felt about myself. Needless to say, my self-esteem took a major hit when I was fired from nearly every job I had in 2020 and I was forced to accomplish . . . absolutely nothing. Unless you count weeping in my pajamas while eating an entire tray of cinnamon rolls an accomplishment.

Because I wasn't allowed to work, I was experiencing all sorts of rock-bottom feelings about myself. When everything tied to your sense of self-worth is no longer present, your world can get seriously shaken. So I did a lot of soul-searching. I thought about my values, and the things that bring me true joy, and I started to wonder why I needed to be achieving something in order to feel good about myself. That all seemed kind of toxic. I don't want to knock the girlboss ideal completely. It *is* badass and important when a woman can take care of herself, achieve everything she wants, and get a Chloé Drew bag with the hard-earned money she got from running her own company or kicking ass at her first-ever job.

It's just that it's easy to get caught in that cycle of needing and wanting to do *more* and work *harder*, and before you know it you're on a treadmill of ambition and it's hard to jump off. And I *hate* treadmills. Unless it's a NordicTrack and I'm doing an iFit walk where I can explore haunted locations in London, or I'm hiking in Scotland with a character from *Outlander*. Even then, I'd rather just watch the show from my couch.

Once I knew that I couldn't (and shouldn't) place so much value on girlbossing, I started looking for other ways to boost my morale. It's going to sound extra cheesy, but I decided to shift my focus to the things I was grateful for. I was pregnant with Hartford, and my lifelong dream had been to become a mom—a mom who also had a career. So I focused on how lucky I was to be pregnant, to have a home, to have a supportive partner. I even focused on the little things like having an iced coffee in the morning, or the utter joy of indulging in marathon binges of *Downton Abbey*. I decided to try something new, to embrace the slowing down of life. I found ways to take pleasure in it. Once I shifted my way of thinking, it was so clear to me just how overrated girlboss culture was. Why do we constantly have to be on top? Sometimes landing somewhere in the middle is the sweetest spot. What's wrong with being happy in the middle? The word *content* no longer scared me. I embraced the feeling of contentment. Looking back, it's pretty shocking to me that I didn't panic more often. I had to embrace this quiet life in order to carry on. Maybe I was delusional, but it worked.

There is a big difference between American girlbossing and the European version. I would so much rather have the European version with hours-long lunches and an obligatory monthlong vacation. A required siesta in Spain in the middle of the day? Six weeks of paid vacation? Free childcare and health insurance? Like, what's that like? I want to live la dolce vita, where life is to be enjoyed and not endured.

And then, right during the exact time I was getting the ick from girlboss culture, the rest of the world was too. It might have had something to do with that whole pandemic thing. We were all forced to slow down that year in a big way. I started googling things like "Can we really have it all?" Or "Is the girlboss dead?" And then, sure enough, my social media algorithms started showing me content from all the *other* women out there who were having the same epiphanies. Women were tired. *I* was tired. While we were all itching to resume our normal lives, we collectively started to really enjoy or accept a slower-paced life. Instead of videos about manifesting success, my TikTok feed was filled with things like "cottagecore," which was about this fantasy of giving up the hustle and bustle of city life and settling down in the countryside and enjoying nature. Basically, beautiful women would post photos wearing flowy prairie dresses as they picked tomatoes on their quaint multimillion-dollar farmsteads.

Throwing it back to Marie Antoinette, as I often do, this new trend reminded me of her Petit Trianon days. At that time, she was over the court life and the responsibilities of Versailles, and she wanted a simple way of living, so she spent time in the little château called the Petit Trianon, aka "the little pleasure palace." This is slightly misleading, since this château would be a mansion to most of the world, but for her it was actually quaint. At the Petit Trianon, she was doing her version of cottagecoring and scaling back. She was steps away from her hamlet, which mimicked a small French farming village with a little pond, vegetable gardens, and farm animals.

During the pandemic, when everyone was longing for air and space, the amount of people I know who moved out of Los Angeles so they could have a proper house with a proper yard somewhere else was astronomical. My husband, Beau, and I even discussed moving, almost daily. If I wasn't going to engage in this hustle culture anymore, then what was the point of living in Los Angeles, a place where everything is so expensive? Could we scale down *everything*, including our city? In the end, we decided to stay because— who am I kidding?—cottagecore is not for me, and I love the Grove too much to ever leave. I could do that cottagecore life for a few months out of the year, but I could never fully commit to baking my own bread and wearing billowy paisley dresses every day for the rest of my life, at least not yet. Ask me again in ten years. Who knows, I might be happily growing tomatoes and pickling carrots in the Italian countryside. I'll be wearing muted, monochromatic outfits, though. No paisley.

Scaling back seems to be the thing now. One simple Google search reveals that the internet is flooded with articles about the death of the girlboss. Since researching the girlboss instead of being one, I've come to learn about her problematic ways. Not only has the term come to be associated with a cheugy Karen-like persona who tries to lure you into multilevel marketing schemes by selling under-eye cream or sketchy vitamin packets, many women have realized that it can encourage unrealistic expectations, and even promote toxic work environments. We all were expected to not only build brands from the ground up but to also be the face of the brand, have a high social media following, and maintain the right image to keep that girlboss idea alive. Looking back, it's kind of wild to think we were just all expected to girlboss. Not everyone wants to or is meant for "bossing." If every single person in the world was a boss, then the world wouldn't work properly. There are so many important career paths to take that make the world a better place that *don't* involve being a boss or having a boss mentality.

Let's take, for example, *Gossip Girl*'s Serena van der Woodsen or *Gilmore Girls* matriarch Emily Gilmore. We can't all be boss bitches like Blair Waldorf, and some of us don't want to do it all on our own like Lorelai Gilmore. But Serena is just as valuable a player as Blair, and Emily is hands down my favorite *Gilmore Girls* character. And Charlotte York from *Sex and the City* gave up her art dealer career to stay home and raise a family! Yes, I know in the latest season of *And Just Like That . . .* she goes back to her job, but it's one of the worst shows ever and doesn't actually count in my eyes. I like to believe that all the girls are still just getting back from Abu Dhabi and Samantha is still besties with everyone.

The problem with me backing away from this mentality is that my nickname as a kid was literally Bossy Stassi. So as much as I try to chill and separate from that side of myself . . . I *am* myself. I can't totally escape it.

Before 2020 hit, I was LITERALLY doing speaking engagements about being a boss, you guys. Can you even? Like, "Hi, I'm such a pro at this girlboss thing that I'm teaching you about it."

And if that weren't cringey enough, my second book was going to be about being a boss bitch. I was going to wear a suit jacket on the cover and everything, because nothing says girlboss like a freakin' Zara blazer. Honestly, it's so embarrassing to think back on—just end me right now, bury me, write my obituary, because I never want to think about it again. I *really* thought I was building this untouchable basic bitch empire. Which is hysterical given the way my 2020 turned out. You could definitely say I "girlbossed a little too close to the sun." I got too confident, too cocky. It's like the morning after a night of drinking on a vacation. You wake up, and you're like, "Holy shit, I'm not that hungover!" You get ambitious, make plans, have a day drink, and then your hangover hits you around 2:00 p.m. and you end up spending the rest of the day puking in your bathroom. Whenever I had one of those days, I'd always joke that I was too cocky that morning. I thought I was invincible. That's basically the equivalent of my 2019 girlboss year.

Now that I have spent this whole chapter pretty much knocking this type of woman, we can still learn a thing or two from the girlboss. They're confident, smart, passionate, hardworking, and, dare I say . . . a little bit delusional? We could all use a tiny bit of delusion in our lives. I personally love BDE, big delusional energy. (*Not* to be confused with big dick energy.) My friend Hannah Berner came up with the term *big delusional energy*. Before I embarked on my 2023 podcast tour, I called her for advice, because she's a comedian who was once on Bravo and continued on to do sold-out nationwide comedy tours. I hadn't toured since before the Canceling, and I needed all the reassurance and wisdom I could get. She told me to channel my BDE, and I immediately understood without needing any explanation of what that meant. But for the sake of this book, I'll explain.

It helps to be a little bit delusional and have an overly confident, inflated sense of self to get certain things done. Plus it's harmless. I mean, a dash of delusion never hurt anybody, right? Basically, you *want* to exaggerate your sense of self-worth, your power, your confidence, your knowledge. I 100 percent needed to channel my BDE to walk back out onstage without fearing that people were there to throw tomatoes at me. And turns out, a little delusion goes a long way. It helped immensely. I was way more nervous for my 2019 and 2020 shows than I ever was for my most recent tour. BDE is vital, and a good thing about the girlboss is that she mastered BDE without ever realizing it. BDE doesn't just help with accomplishing something, it helps in social situations, it helps with your mental health, it helps with your overall day-to-day life. If you walk into a friend's party with BDE, that social anxiety you might have is a tad diminished. Let's say you're feeling a little less-than after scrolling Instagram for a couple of hours. That BDE will serve as a reminder that you're badass, and it'll help get you out of that funk. It just makes it a little harder for things to get you down when you've got that BDE. So while we're pretty much done with the girlboss trope, we can still take a few ideals from them. The girlboss isn't all bad, just a little misguided.

I will always be someone who likes doing the most; that's just a part of my nature. But the difference now lies in the fact that I don't feel *pressure* to do the most. I don't feel like I need to do the most in order to feel a sense of self-worth or identity. My identity revolves around so many different things now. There are the big things like mother, wife, podcaster, writer, but there are also the little things that are just as important, such as period-piece fanatic, lover of gold jewelry and beige OOTDs, haunted house aficionado, avid online shopper, travel enthusiast, happy hour supporter, Raven-claw member, person with a past life as a shoemaker at Versailles in the eighteenth century . . . just to name a few. All of these things make me feel great about myself because they are so authentically me, and they bring joy to my life. I feel my self-worth cup fill up when I'm extra patient with my daughter and son, when I'm communicative with Beau, when a podcast guest tells me that I made them feel so comfortable during the episode, and when a Khaleesi comes up to me and tells me one of my books got her through a really hard time in her life. I've even learned how to feel great about myself on my lazy days where I don't wash my face or bother to get dressed. I've found joy in the littlest things that don't involve even a grain of hustle culture.

Being a boss is *not* the only true marker of success. It feels like there are so many strict rules surrounding what it means to be a girlboss, that if you don't hit each point on the checklist, you feel like a failure. Not everyone's personality type is meant for CEO life or influencer life, and that's okay. I guess what I'm saying is, I give all of us permission to chill.

Ultimate Girlbosses

Now, I love a good list, and this chapter wouldn't feel complete without my list of women who epitomized girlboss energy. I want to preface this by saying, despite the recent negativity surrounding the girlboss, I still admire boss energy. All the following women have incredible boss energy, some good, some not so good. But I would like to give the following women (whom I respect) permission to chill, just a little bit . . .

* **ANY FASHION BLOGGER YOU'VE EVER FOLLOWED:** I mean, these women HUSTLE. It may look like their lives are so easy and glamorous, but they have to document nearly every moment, and I mean every moment. Every makeup application, every outfit, every party, every flight, every hotel room, every moment they're feeling anything that may make them seem more relatable. Lol. I mean, do they ever just stay home and do nothing?

* **KIM KARDASHIAN:** There are actual story lines on *Keeping Up with the Kardashians* about how Kim is a ridiculously hardworking overachiever who, according to Kourtney, isn't ever happy with what she has and always wants more. And who can forget her iconic "Get your f*cking ass up and work" response when she was interviewed by *Variety*

and was asked to give advice to women in business? "Get your f*cking ass up and work. It seems like nobody wants to work these days." Icon.

✳ **DAENERYS TARGARYEN:** Talk about someone who girl-bossed a little too close to the sun. She could've used a medieval Xanax or two.

✳ **HERMIONE GRANGER:** Definitely a know-it-all, always has to be doing the most in school. I would imagine to Hermione, an A is a failure as it's not an A+.

✳ **MIRANDA PRIESTLY:** I don't even feel like this one needs an explanation. She really needed a good hug.

✳ **RIHANNA:** Not only is her Super Bowl performance one of the most watched in history, but she performed pregnant on elevated platforms in the freaking sky, and paused to apply some of her own Fenty Beauty powder to her perfect face, making it the most iconic commercial for a product, like ever. Genius. Did I mention she's a billionaire?

✳ **SAMANTHA JONES:** "I love you but I love me more" is the ultimate girlboss slogan.

✳ **JENNIFER LOPEZ:** JLo, I love you and I give you permission to do less. Take a break, go on vacay, stay home and binge a show. I watched her documentary three times and cried every single time. I'm in awe of her work ethic and passion. But, seriously, she deserves a little breaky break, which she seems to get now with Ben, since they're always photographed laughing on vacation. Good for you, girl.

✳ **EMILY IN PARIS:** Insufferable, yet kinda likable? She has MAJOR big delusional energy. And she definitely would've captioned a photo "Too inspired to be tired."

When I think of a typical girlboss, my brain instantly goes to a micro influencer who sends out mass DMs urging her followers to "get out of their own way" and start making moves working for LuLaRoe. You know the one. Her messages always start with "Hey, hon . . ." She captions her IG vacation photos with "Out. Of. Office." Her laptop has that millennial-pink hard-shell case, and her desk wouldn't be complete without all the gold office accessories from Target. (Side note: I own a lot of the gold Target office accessories. Again, the cheugy girlboss, while I cringe at her, is still a part of who *I* am.)

Typical Girlboss

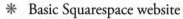

* Basic Squarespace website

* Blazers (I live in blazers)

* Iced matcha . . . half almond/half oat (one of my go-to drinks)

YOUR CLASSIC GIRL BOSS BLAZER (OBVI OVERSIZED)

* Regular Drybar blowouts (I must have gotten forty-eight blowouts in 2019)

* Pearls

* Gucci loafers (I own these and love them)

* Aesthetically pleasing desk, with gold accessories

* Planner

* Business casual outfits

* Takes OOTDs

* Meditates every morning for five minutes on her Calm app

* Pinot grigio

SO CLASSIC.
SO CHIC.

GIRLBOSSING
EVERY DAY

MY WEEK

MON	TUES	WED
9-5 VERY Big meeting!	12:00 GIRL LUNCH	11:00 NAILS

THURS	FRI	SAT
9-5 more meetings!	HAPPY HOUR	SPA DAY!! / SUN

* Always has a manicure (a rule I live by)

* Worships Taylor Swift and Beyoncé (rightfully so, we all should)

Takeaway

Maybe girlbossing will never (and should never) totally go away, because women being able to work, vote, run empires, and have their own credit cards are important advancements. I'm trying to accept that taking the pressure off does not mean you are failing, and that BDE (big delusional energy) is key when you're feeling less-than-bossy. If you find yourself feeling guilty for taking a break or a nap or just not wanting to kill it all the damn time, tell yourself that no one can girlboss 24-7, and that soft life might not be so bad.

CHAPTER 2

Here Comes the Bride
(Just Not Like She Planned)

*Y*ou were supposed to be at my wedding. Okay, maybe not *in person*, but you were going to be there in spirit, via Bravo and *Vanderpump Rules*, since we'd planned a whole giant extravaganza in Rome that would have been filmed and televised for anyone who wanted to watch. We rented out a huge estate for the production team plus 150 guests. You (yes, you!) were going to see a band, a glass tent (because indoor girlies like to enjoy nature—within reason), fireworks, and multiple outfit changes. It was going to be a dream wedding, but then 2020 came along.

Before we go any further, I want to say that the wedding I ended up having *was* a dream. I am extremely fortunate to have had my Italian wedding with a beautiful dress and Aperol spritzes all around. Did you know that you can drink 163 Aperol spritzes in Italy over the course of a single day and never feel hungover? It's absolutely true. So the wedding I had was gorgeous and perfect and a dream—it just wasn't what I had planned when I was in my "I *can* have it all" state of mind, before reality came crashing in. *Actual* reality, not TV reality.

In case you didn't hear, everything was shut down in 2020—including my career, my life, and my self-esteem. Because of my past actions, I was canceled, fired from the show, fired from everything. Obviously, that dream televised Italian wedding would be canceled along with everything else. I wrote about this experience in detail in my last book, and I own that I screwed up big-time. I'm proud of how much I've grown and learned. I also need to acknowledge that so many people went through experiences *so much worse than mine* during that horrible time. I'm not here begging for you to pity me, I'm just telling you what happened in case you've never been exposed to social media or tabloids and you don't already know just through pop culture osmosis. If you're one of those people, hello and welcome to my life!

It never even occurred to me that I could potentially *not* have my wedding televised. When you're on a show for as long as I was, it's strange to think of a big event not being filmed. It was the norm for me. If I went to brunch and there wasn't a camera, it felt like something was seriously off. Is my wallet missing? Did I forget to brush my teeth? Did I blow out all the candles so the house doesn't burn down? Nope, just a lack of cameras! If I fought with a friend and a producer wasn't capturing our teary arguments, what was I even doing there? Most of my adult life was spent on *Vanderpump*

Rules. All my major moments—whether great or not so great/ absolutely mortifying and/or horrible—were on the show. This big TV wedding was going to be my happy-ending princess moment. Like a fairy tale, it was meant to be.

Like many so-called girlbosses—Elle Woods, Tracy Flick, or any character played by Reese Witherspoon, really—when I do things, I like to really *do things*. This probably won't come as a shock to anyone who has seen me on TV or peeked at my Instagram Stories for five seconds. I mean, we've seen this with my birthdays year after year. I like to make things a big deal. If there is a theme, I lean way in. Costume party? I've already got three elaborate options, at least. If there's an opportunity to exert some main-character energy, I'm more than ready to go. Have you seen how I decorate my house for Halloween? I am not playing around. Every Halloween, I cover all the normal, non-scary art in our house with portraits of terrifying historical figures. I might cover a flowery still life with a picture of Elizabeth Báthory, the most prolific female serial killer who ever existed. She actually bathed in her victims' blood. Total vampire vibes. That might sound over the top to some people, but to me it's just necessary. I mean, it's Halloween. It's not the type of holiday that begs for subtlety.

Side note: Whether it's Halloween or a random day in February, I fully believe that every single person should live with main-character energy. I've said it before and I'll say it again—if you don't consider yourself to be the Beyoncé of your own life, then what is the point of anything?! You are the main character of your life, so relish in that. I don't mean live as if you're the center of the universe (ew), but don't go through life acting like a background actor. Get in there.

So, clearly I like to be festive and do it up, and weddings are prime time to do it up. Given that I had spent the majority of my adult life on *Vanderpump Rules*, and that viewers had witnessed all of my important life moments, every failed relationship, every meltdown, every triumph—this wedding was going to be my *ultimate* moment. I know how Bravo watchers can be (I mean, I'm one of them). We watch these televised weddings and pick every single detail apart. Nothing is off-limits, even the napkins. Napkins say a lot about a person! I love a monogrammed wedding napkin, but if I see a cheesy saying on a napkin like "Booze and Bad Dance Moves" or "Till Death Do Us Party," I'm out. I will very seriously consider vacating the premises.

Before the Canceling of 2020, I knew that it was my choice to put my wedding out there, so any judgments I received for it would be fair game. In true Stassi fashion, I obsessively perfected every over-the-top, unnecessary detail. My intention was to have the most elegant, special wedding we'd seen on Bravo. Like a true psychopath, I studied Kim Kardashian's *Keeping Up with the Kardashians* wedding episode on repeat for months to get in the spirit. She had her rehearsal dinner at Versailles, my actual favorite place on earth, a place I'm 99.9 percent sure I lived at in a past life. Supposedly she flew everyone to Italy on private jets for the wedding ceremony, where she had *the* Andrea Bocelli sing as she walked down the aisle. I mean, how baller do you have to be to rent out VERSAILLES? Goals.

Initially, we were going to have 150 people at Villa Miani in Rome. The villa sits on Rome's highest hill, Monte Mario, and it overlooks the entire city. It dates back to 1837. 1837! Imagine the ghosts. We had rented out the entire villa so that the production crew could fully take over the place. It's a big deal to rent out this entire villa. I would venture to say that no one is taking over this location without a five-hundred-person guest list, that's how large it is. We knew we wanted as much of the wedding to be outdoors as possible, because the view is nothing short of spectacular. It would be insulting to be indoors. Because of that, we wanted a giant glass tent to be built on the grounds in case of weather issues. I had been speaking with our producers about how I wanted everything to take place at night, including our vows, so the lighting was every-thing. I wanted outdoor chandeliers everywhere, elegant twinkle lights placed about meticulously. And don't even get me started on the fireworks.

I knew I wanted fireworks the second I saw that image of Harry and Meghan at their wedding reception with their backs to the camera, just looking up at the display. I couldn't be more of a basic bitch if I tried. I had gotten two wedding dresses from Galia Lahav (Beyoncé wore one of her dresses for her vow renewal, so naturally I was obsessed). One for the ceremony, and then obviously, I mean, *obviously*, a dress change for the reception. I wanted to splurge on flowers. I knew I wanted ivory flowers with lush greenery, and I wanted them everywhere. There was going to be a band playing for our reception because there is nothing more fun than live music at a wedding. Basically, this wedding was going to be intense. As I'm

OVER-THE-TOP FIREWORKS

writing this, I'm cringing over how bratty and demanding I sound, but I'm just trying to paint an honest picture of what I was planning for my televised wedding. Maybe I was getting a little, just a *little*, carried away. For someone who never dreamed about a princess wedding as a kid, I definitely made up for lost time.

The wedding I ended up having, while it wasn't what I had initially intended, was one of the best days and experiences of my life. There were no producers telling me I had to film with certain people, or that I had to schedule things in a way I had no control over. I got to relax and be present and truly enjoy every moment. And no, I was not a Bridezilla. I swear! The Dark Passenger—my diabolical alter ego—did not emerge once. Ask Beau!

The day after my wedding, I was talking to one of the *Vander-pump* producers who had attended and he made a joke about how he wished he could've filmed it. When I immediately replied, "Absolutely not," I think he was a little shocked, since a year before I had been all about filming it. But I got to spend my wedding morning exactly how I wanted to, which was by myself in my hotel room, having eggs Benedict and iced tea, looking out at the city of Rome. (Fun fact: In Italy you only get one egg with eggs Benedict, so I guess it's technically egg Benedict.) I sat there for a long time just soaking in all the peace I felt. I thought about my life, about Beau, about our daughter, Hartford. I got to have a very important moment with myself. And after I told the producer this, he was like, "Yeah, you definitely wouldn't have been able to do that if we were filming."

Instead, I would've been forced to get ready with a bunch of friends (I mean, not the worst thing in the world), and I would've been forced to talk about whatever drama was going on with them at the time (not as fun). I'd have to get mic'd up and wait around for people to do their walk-ups, which is where they come in and I pretend I didn't know they would be walking in at that exact moment. Surprise! I would've had to invite people I didn't actually care to have there because I would have been scared that not inviting them would be seen as making some sort of statement, thus causing more drama. The day would've felt chaotic, and it wouldn't have been the day I wanted it to be. The day that I actually ended up having without the cameras was pure love and magic.

Before it became pure love and magic though, I had to scale it the *eff* down.

You know how in the *Sex and the City* movie, Carrie's wedding starts getting bigger and more extravagant, and she blames it on the wedding dress? I blame my vision of an Italian princess wedding with fireworks and a glass tent on the fact that it was going to be televised. The pressure was on, and I wanted to deliver an epic wedding not just for myself and Beau but for *Vanderpump Rules* viewers as well.

Given that I had just been fired from every job I had, I wasn't able to plan for a wedding of that size, so we knew we had to cut the guest list. That was the hardest part of the whole process. We went back and forth with our wedding planner on how we wanted to do this. Yes, we were cutting costs, but the wedding planner had already been paid. Plus, I don't speak Italian, so planning a wedding in Italy would have involved me using freetranslation.com to describe a floral arrangement. So the question was, did we want a seventy-five-person wedding and cut back in other places? Or did we want a fifteen-person wedding but make it a full-blown experience for those people? We eventually settled on around thirty people. The thirty people who were closest to us, the thirty people who stuck around after 2020 to be in our lives as a couple and a family. Because we had already committed to renting out the whole giant villa, Beau and I joked that our wedding was going to be like having a tiny picnic in the 70,240-seat SoFi Stadium. Actually, that is probably Beau's dream wedding scenario.

It wasn't just the guest list that needed to be cut. We needed to cut back wherever we could. That meant definitely no fireworks, no outdoor chandeliers (we didn't even do twinkle lights), no glass tent. I wore my main wedding dress the whole night (I know, I know, woe is me) and used my reception dress as my rehearsal dinner dress to avoid having to purchase another gown. I made sure white flowers with greenery were used only when absolutely necessary. I mean, sometimes flowers *are* necessary. The way I saw it, the location and view were so stunning, we might as well let that shine and be the star of the wedding, so to speak.

I was so worried, but it ended up being infinitely more spectacular than I imagined. I loved that everyone could roam the entire villa without running into guests from another wedding or party. It felt like we were a small group who had the *Beauty and the Beast* castle all to ourselves. And because our guest list was so small, everyone knew one another, or had at least already gotten to know one another and hung out at our welcome dinner the night before, so it truly felt like one big happy family. Beau and I never felt like we had to make the rounds and exchange pleasantries with guests, because we had already all been hanging out. Everyone was able to just relax, drink endless amounts of wine, and have fun. *Highly* recommend a small wedding.

When it came to my wedding dresses, I ended up realizing that I would've hated doing an outfit change. First of all, I would've had to leave the party to go change and get ready again. That just seems like a huge waste of time. I would be missing out on precious seconds of fun! I would have had FOMO at my own wedding. Second, I loved both of my wedding dresses so much that I was happy that each of them got to be worn for an entire night. Both dresses got their moments. The villa was so spectacular that a glass tent would have been unnecessary. I mean, if it's ever *necessary*, I don't know. And the tables and tablescape for thirty people ended up looking straight out of *Vogue* Weddings. It was very Marie Antoinette during that "low-key" Petit Trianon phase. The French country elements oddly blended in perfectly with the outdoor area of the Italian villa. The tables were set up in one big U-shape, and we ate the best cacio e pepe I had ever had, among other things like caprese and beef filet. Like I said, I am not complaining. At all.

It was intimate yet still felt so grand and of another time. Instead of having a wedding cake, we did a limoncello shot toast for everyone before we opened the dance floor. I had spent weeks if not months creating the perfect playlist. I am a huge believer in the importance of a soundtrack. It sets the tone and vibe, and transports you in a way no other element of a party can.

Beau and I had originally wanted to book this musical duo 2CELLOS for our televised wedding. We love an instrumental cello sound, especially when it's with modern songs. Obviously with cutting back on the cost, booking the world famous 2CELLOS wasn't going to be an option, so we opted to make a playlist with instrumental modern songs. Now, I know what you're thinking. You're thinking, so basically the *Bridgerton* soundtrack, right? And you would be somewhat correct. Yes, the musical vibe was the exact same one that *Bridgerton* made popular, but let me just credit myself and Beau real fast and say that we had wanted to do this with 2CELLOS in 2019, before *Bridgerton* was released. Honestly I don't know why I care so much that people might think I copied *Bridgerton*. I freaking love *Bridgerton*. I am obsessed with it, in fact. My ringtone is the *Bridgerton* theme song. I might as well just lean into it, and say my wedding soundtrack was very freaking *Bridgerton*.

As our guests rolled in, they were greeted with our favorite Aperol spritzes and *Bridgerton* music all around. It was the vibe of my dreams. Beau came out to Vitamin String Quartet's version of "Dancing on My Own." I get the lyrics of the song make it an odd choice, but it's one of our favorite songs, so it made sense for us. Hartford and Katie Maloney walked out to the instrumental version of "Rewrite the Stars" from *The Greatest Showman*, by the Piano Guys. One big mistake I made was not having a bouquet for Katie. I figured I would hand her mine during the ceremony, but I forgot that she needed some flowers to hold as she walked down the aisle! Instead, she had to figure out what to do with her hands while thirty-plus people watched her. Katie, I AM SO FREAKING SORRY. She wasn't mad at me, but I was and am still mad at myself. Forgive me, Katie!

IVORY FLOWERS

Bouquet in hand, I went the traditional route, walking out to "Canon in D Major" (string quartet). And for our recessional song, Beau and I picked a string quartet version of Pitbull's "Give Me Everything," because, well, duh, Pitbull is life. After the ceremony, we transitioned the music to what I like to call "Italian Rat Pack vibes." I wanted everyone to feel like they were in a classic Italian film during our cocktail hour and dinner. We first danced to "Nothing Can Change This Love" by Sam Cooke. And for the dance portion of the reception, it was what you would normally expect to hear at weddings. But our last song of the night was really special: Mariah Carey's "All I Want for Christmas Is You." Christmas music at a wedding in Italy in May? Yes, I can see how that would be weird. But it was so utterly and completely perfect. I mean, name a better song. So while we didn't get to have a live band, we poured so much of our hearts and time into curating the perfect playlist that represented us, and the DJ delivered it all flawlessly. Not joking, I had so many guests asking me for the playlist link because they were so in love with it.

We didn't make any concrete after-party plans for our wedding. Beau and I just figured we'd all tipsily make our way into some cool small Italian bar and shut the place down, Rat Pack style. I would still be in my wedding dress, obviously. But on the day of the wedding, one of my oldest and best friends in the whole world, Alex Stafford, texted me about her family hosting an after-party. Her parents were also there for our wedding (I grew up with them, and Beau adores them), and they had checked into their hotel to find that they had been upgraded to a hotel room that was essentially an entire floor. It looked like it was straight out of an Italian version of *Downton Abbey*. It felt like you were in a palace. There was so much old-world charm, it was almost museum-like. And their room had a massive balcony wrapping around the whole place. There was even a library with actual books from the 1800s—like how have they never been stolen before? I fully asked every single one of my friends if they would do the honors and steal one for me, because the thought of becoming a thief on my wedding night and getting thrown into an Italian jail seriously disturbed me. Sadly, no one honored my request. Now that I think about it though, I love that all our friends were so morally compassed.

I wouldn't have been able to dream up a more ideal after-party. When I realized it was 3:30 a.m., I couldn't believe I had lasted that long. As Beau and I were leaving, we saw a group of our guests sitting at this huge round table underneath a dome in one of the living areas doing a séance, conducted by our friend Taylor Donohue. She isn't a professional, but she sometimes does this when she's drunk. I mean, what a fitting way for our wedding night to end. A creepy séance! It was very on-brand for me. If we had been filming our wedding for *Vanderpump*, we never would've been allowed to have that after-party. Everything is scheduled far in advance when you're filming, because it takes a long time to get clearance to film at locations. You can't just bring the cameras and crew wherever you want. Instead of a party with a séance, I would have been crying in a hotel room in my wedding dress, fighting with someone from the cast (probably).

I watched all these Gen Z TikToks that said weddings were cheugy and outdated, so I can't imagine how Hartford's generation will feel about them. Are weddings as we know them today on the way out? I understand the argument that they're ridiculously expensive, and that the money could be spent traveling for a year, or on a down payment for a home. That is an incredibly valid argument. I feel very Libra when it comes to weddings (even though I'm a Cancer with Capricorn rising and a Scorpio moon)—I weigh all the different sides. I think that weddings are such a personal thing; there are no right or wrong answers. Could we have put the money we spent on our wedding toward our home? Yes. But I have zero, and I mean zero, regrets over the wedding we ended up having. We have those memories to always look back on together. Life is all about moments and making memories, and that day is really up there in terms of good memories.

There are very few major events in life where there is an opportunity to show people who you are, what you are about, and where you're at in life in such a big celebratory way. A wedding is typically the major life event to do that, so it makes sense as to why we get so wrapped up in the perfection of it all. Side note: When you think back on your grandparents or ancestors, it's always the wedding photo that's used to represent someone after they've passed away. I totally get that this is morbid, but bear with me. Most people will have one or two main photos that will survive them and keep their legacy going after they've died. I call these "ghost photos," the ones that will live on to represent a person. Almost always, one of those photos is a wedding photo. I have my grandmother's wedding photo on a bookshelf, and my mom has these crazy-old creepy Victorian photos of my Swedish relatives, all from weddings. So how can we *not* put pressure on ourselves to look our absolute freaking best on our wedding day, when it might be the one photo that survives for our great-great-great-grandchildren to see?!

We put all this pressure on ourselves to have the perfect wedding. It's one of those rare things in life that is supposedly only going to happen for you once, so you better nail it. Add in the addition of social media and the comment section. It always comes back to social media. I mean, people will pick apart every last detail. The comment sections on wedding-related posts scare me almost as much as mom-shamers. And this isn't a celebrity thing. This is an every-person thing. People you went to high school with are going to see your wedding posts and start a group chat with their friends about whether your dress was tacky or ill-fitting. Your coworkers are going to have opinions about the hair and makeup. Everyone is going to dissect every detail on social media (or behind your back), and you'll probably be getting your ghost photo out of it. So yeah, the pressure is on.

The wedding we had wasn't what we planned, but it was better. In the end, we could have been eating off of paper plates and I would have been fine. Well . . . probably not, but you know what I'm saying. If it had all been televised, Scheana would have been encouraged to say something negative about my dress because in season three of the show I had *lots* to say about her dress, so it would have been fair game, and I would have totally understood. (It's easy for me to say this now because it didn't actually happen.) We also wouldn't have been able to stay in my dream hotel, because production would have wanted a good deal, so we would have stayed in a resort hotel across town. It's not exactly woe is me, but to me Rome isn't about sipping mai tais by a pool. It's about staying at Hotel de Russie and sipping an Aperol spritz while strolling in their freaking SECRET GARDEN. For real, they have a secret garden on the grounds. Also, who knows who we would have caught having a secret affair! Raquel wasn't invited because we've never been good friends, so there wouldn't have been any drama in that sense, unless I was pressured to invite her and James for the show. Also, if 2020 never happened and I had had my "dream" wedding on *Vanderpump Rules*, Jax and Brittany would have actually shown up.

About that . . .

I get asked about what happened between Brittany/Jax and me/Beau all the time. So here you go. They were of course invited, because they were two of our close friends. They RSVP'd yes, but I didn't hear much from Brittany leading up to the wedding, which was weird because usually you're texting about being excited or asking what clothes you're packing or *something*. Not only that, we started hearing from Beau's best friend, Rob, that Jax was texting him and Tom Schwartz saying they might not go to the wedding, and listing off reasons why. One reason was that Jax doesn't like Europe. WHAT?! It's an entire continent! Anyway, this was weeks before the actual date, after they had RSVP'd they were coming. A yes RSVP isn't a maybe, it's a "definite yes unless something drastic happens." I'm not saying they *had* to fly to Italy. I get that it's a lot to ask, but if they weren't going to come they could have told us, and we could have invited two people who wanted to be there. A little communication would have been nice, is what I'm saying.

After the pandemic and so many months of not knowing

whether we would get to celebrate in a big way at all, it was not easy to keep the guest list small. It pained us to *not* be able to invite people we cared about. So this wasn't a petty thing for us, it was deeply painful. Imagine if two of your closest friends just . . . didn't want to come?

Two weeks before the wedding we told them we'd heard that they weren't coming and said it was hurtful to hear it from other people. Jax denied everything at first, like he always does. When I told him we had texts from him saying they weren't coming, he was like, *Okay you're right* . . . BUT HE STILL SAID THEY WERE COMING. Then the day we're flying to Italy, a few hours before I'm supposed to leave for the airport, Brittany sends a long text explaining that they aren't coming. It was such a slap in the face. They were supposed to be our ride-or-die friends, and this felt like they didn't respect that friendship at all. Their wedding in Kentucky had to be the most important thing in our lives for an entire summer when we were filming the show. We were there for all of it. As soon as I read that text, Beau and I were like, we're done. I wasn't going to just roll over for this one. My main issue is with Jax, because I feel Brittany would have wanted to come, plus she wasn't texting a bunch of people about it. Lala Kent couldn't come because she was on a podcast tour, and I'm not angry with her *because she told us.* She didn't pretend she was coming, talk shit behind our backs, and then cancel at the last minute.

It didn't help that after this happened, they kept going on podcasts and talking about it. On Scheana's podcast, she and Brittany ripped into me and my wedding. They kept talking to press and telling people that Beau and I were holding a grudge because they weren't coming to the wedding, which wasn't true. Many people couldn't come to our wedding, but they told us in advance, and didn't pretend they were coming until the last minute. This just pushed me and Beau further away from them. What it boils down to is this: I've obviously been burned by Jax more times than I can count. On *Vanderpump Rules*, we called it "being Jax'd." You can just go to old episodes and see for yourself. This time Jax was doing it to Beau, after I had encouraged their friendship. Why would I continue a friendship when someone has repeatedly shown me his character? Nope. Not anymore. I want to surround myself with people I can count on. Brittany and I are cordial when we see each other at the occasional birthday party; Jax has sent Beau texts asking him to bury the hatchet and come hang out at Jax's bar. That one gave me a good laugh.

I know that, as I write this, they have split up, so I wish them the best. That doesn't mean what they did is right though.

We—meaning everyone—shouldn't have to put up with people hurting us. It goes back to claiming that main-character energy. I get that people make mistakes. Fights happen, but this was different. Our first "wedding" was us signing papers during my baby shower. Italy was *the wedding*. Getting older means realizing you can't have it all, that friends will sometimes disappoint you, and that you don't have to put up with being hurt. I don't want to say I would never forgive them, because I've made that mistake in the past and that sentiment always comes back to haunt me. If I felt like they were genuinely sorry, I would absolutely forgive.

I bet Bravo would have *died* to film all that drama. Besides that, there wasn't much chaos for them to capture. Except for Beau and the fish.

Beau and I went back and forth about whether we should have a fish option. I fully realize this doesn't qualify as a major decision that would impact global peace, but it was more money, so we debated it. We decided to add the fish option, but the night of our wedding, Beau sat there stewing at our table, going, "They didn't bring out the fish. They can't get away with this!" He was pissed. It was a whole ordeal (for Beau) and to this day, if I say, "I can't believe we got married at a villa in Italy with our closest friends, it

was so magical . . ." his response will be, "Yeah but they forgot to bring out the fish!"

So in addition to two of our best friends flaking, me forgetting to give Katie a bouquet (I'm sorry again!), and some paparazzi lurking around and trying to post wedding photos before we got a chance to do it, the day was not what I originally planned, but it was better than I could have ever dreamed. If it had been as planned, I probably would have leaned in to the Bridezilla vibe for the show because I was so used to being the Birthdayzilla for so long. It's almost like a "give the people what they want" sort of thing. There would have been a storyline of me being a bridal monster and it would have been *real.*

I can just see a plotline where Beau and his friends want to go out and I turn into the Dark Passenger. It wouldn't have been fake, but reality show producers know how to stir the pot or plant a seed that ends up growing into a disaster. It would have been on their checklist:

Get footage of Stassi getting ready, plus tons of gossip.

Film close-ups of the food, plus people talking shit.

Make sure Stassi goes full Dark Passenger by the end of the night.

Instead, I was the most relaxed bride you have ever seen. I swear. My idea of "having it all" for my wedding shifted, and we downsized, we adapted. In the end, my televised princess happy ending turned into a private, magical night with no fireworks, no fish, and no glass tent. It was exactly what I needed. Most important—I got a very good ghost photo.

Wedding Playlist

* "City of Stars" by Mr. & Mrs. Cello

* "With or Without You" by 2CELLOS

* "Come as You Are" by The Hipster Orchestra

* "A Million Dreams" (Violin Instrumental) by Taylor Davis

* "Fly Me to the Moon" by Midnite String Quartet

* "Waiting for a Girl Like You" by Midnite String Quartet

* "Story of My Life" by Midnite String Quartet

* "Hungry Like the Wolf" by Midnite String Quartet

* "Royals" by Vitamin String Quartet

* "Blinding Lights" by Vitamin String Quartet

* "Señorita" by Simply Three

* "We Found Love" by Midnite String Quartet

* "Feel It Still" by Vitamin String Quartet

* "Girls Like You" by Vitamin String Quartet

* "Sweet but Psycho" by Vitamin String Quartet

* "Don't You (Forget About Me)" by Vitamin String Quartet

✳ "We Are Young" by Vitamin String Quartet

✳ "Diamonds" by Hannah V and Joe Rodwell

✳ "Dancing on My Own" by Vitamin String Quartet (Beau walked out to this song.)

✳ "Rewrite the Stars" by the Piano Guys (Katie and Hartford walked to this song.)

✳ "Canon in D Major (String Quartet)" by Johann Pachelbel, Stringspace (My song—yes, it's basic, but it's timeless, 'kay?!)

✳ "Give Me Everything" by Josh Vietti (Our recessional song—had to incorporate Mr. 305 somewhere.)

Takeaway

It's not as if I scaled my wedding down from an Italian villa in Rome to a Buca di Beppo in a strip mall, but I did have to take stock of what really mattered to me, and focus on that. And it was infinitely better. We're so pressured to go big, be bold, outshine, but at the end of the day, do monogrammed tablecloths really matter? The answer is no. No they don't. Relationships matter, good food matters, and glass tents are way overrated.

CHAPTER 3

Women Are Not Rubber Bands! We Don't "Snap Back"

I thought the final month of pregnancy was tough, but that first month after giving birth to Hartford truly shook my world. I was not prepared *at all*, and I blame all those celebrities who look so perfect and serene mere days after giving birth. Love them all, but it should be mandatory for all photos of them to come with a bright red warning label:

WARNING: These photos may bring about deranged, unrealistic ideas about postpartum bodies. View at your own risk!

When I tell you I didn't leave my house for the first six weeks after I gave birth the first time, other than to take Hartford to the doctor and to get newborn photos, I am not joking. I'm not *totally* delusional, so of course I was fully aware that it would take a bit of time for my belly to go back to anything close to what

it had been before it was stretched out by an actual human being living in there (plus all the funfetti cakes I ate), but I was not prepared to gain *more* weight in the months after giving birth. I saw all of these celebrities and influencers give birth, and then within a week, they're out on the town with their Artipoppe baby carriers and flat stomachs peeking out underneath crop tops, or posting photos of themselves in their prepregnancy jeans. WTF!

Before I even gave birth I read message boards about postpartum weight loss, and how most of the weight gain is water weight (yeah, right), or stories about how women lost twenty pounds within the first month. Yes, I know message boards can be insane, but I was desperate for some hope. This all made me way too optimistic as I entered into my postpartum-body journey. This was the one time big delusional energy did not do me any favors.

First of all, why doesn't anyone warn you that you might blow up like an actual blimp after giving birth due to swelling? After the epidural, the IV, and whatever else was pumped into me, I swelled so much that I thought I was going to have to be rehospitalized *after* giving birth. My legs quite literally doubled in size—and it lasted *an entire two weeks*. I know, I know, not the most pressing problem in the world, but STILL! When I brought Hartford to her first pediatrician appointment, the only shoes that fit were my UGG house slippers. They aren't even real shoes! I remember Beau and my manager, Lo, coming up with plans to distract the paparazzi in front of my house so that I could get in the car without being photographed looking like Jabba the Hutt. I'm not somebody who typically has paparazzi parked outside my house, but paparazzi love to stalk someone when one of three things is happening:

1. There is a scandal (murder, cheating, murder *and* cheating, etc.).

2. Someone is pregnant.

3. Someone just gave birth.

The only times I've felt unsafe to leave my house are when the paparazzi are lurking. People are obsessed with women's bodies in general, and specifically during and after pregnancy. Photos of pregnant or postpartum women sell for much more (it's gross, I know). There is this obsession with the "snap back," and people love to pick apart women's bodies and analyze whether they're efficiently "snapping back" in the appropriate amount of time. We're not rubber bands, we're women. Even Emily Ratajkowski. Or maybe she's half woman, half rubber band. The point is, this impossible standard made me painfully insecure. I've always had my insecurities, but this was on a level I've never experienced before. I couldn't stand the way I looked in the mirror, so much so that I actively avoided the mirror. How did Kate Middleton stand on those steps smiling outside the Lindo Wing of St. Mary's Hospital in London EVERY SINGLE TIME she gave birth?! I would have lost my shit.

I know it's not advancing feminism to admit that these things upset me, but I truly looked like Quasimodo after I delivered Hartford. I thought that I would give birth, lose eight pounds of baby, twenty pounds of water, and be into some of my old clothes the next week. It ended up taking me exactly a year to get back to my former self. Because I only got bigger with the swelling after I came home from the hospital, I hid as much as possible. I couldn't even

fit into my pregnancy clothes. I pretty much roamed the house in an oversize robe and adult diapers like some scary updated version of a postpartum Victorian ghost who refuses to leave the house à la that movie *The Others*.

Moral of the story: don't compare yourself to people on social media. Their journeys aren't necessarily going to be your journey. I also think that Instagram influencers/models are just this separate breed of human being that must contain some sort of alien DNA, because that's the only possible explanation that makes sense. Hand me a Nobel Prize in Medicine any time.

Things I Miss About Single Years

＊ Obviously getting more than seven hours of sleep.

＊ Sleeping through the night without waking up every time I hear a noise on the baby monitor.

＊ Sleeping without a baby monitor.

＊ Having someone text and ask if I want to go get brunch/dinner/happy hour, and being able to do that without planning a week ahead of time.

＊ Traveling whenever.

＊ Spending money on only myself.

✳ Impromptu anything at all.

✳ Mimosas for breakfast.

✳ Being caught up on all the good TV shows.

✳ A home free of toys in primary colors and boogers on our coffee table.

✳ When holidays were actually holidays.

✳ Shopping in person without having to rush.

✳ Clutch handbags, so chic, so not possible when you have kids.

✳ Staying up late knowing I can sleep in.

✳ The ability to just leave my house, get in the car, and have it not matter where I go or when I return.

✳ Unplanned sexy time.

✳ Going to the bathroom alone.

✳ Scrolling through my phone in bed in the mornings.

✳ White/ivory coats. Not worth the investment anymore, can't risk the potential stains.

✳ The ability to take my time putting daily OOTDs together.

✳ Hangovers that I could nurse on the couch all day.

I wrote about this in my last book, but the one thing I did try to prepare myself for was postpartum depression. I've always been someone who has struggled with on-and-off anxiety and depression (more on that later), and given everything that I dealt with in 2020, I felt like all those environmental factors that would contribute to depression were present. So throughout my whole pregnancy, I tried to mentally prepare myself for a tough time. Luckily, I ended up never suffering from PPD, but there were many moments of feeling down (which had nothing to do with weight—well, okay, maybe a little), and even more moments of loneliness.

First, breastfeeding was very difficult for me. I had a feeling during my pregnancy that I might have breastfeeding issues since I had gotten a breast reduction/lift years prior, so I had hired a lactation consultant before I gave birth just to get ahead of it. I did all the research and prepared myself as much as I possibly could, but honestly no lesson or guidebook could have properly readied me for that experience. My instincts were right, and I ended up not producing enough milk, so we had to supplement with formula from the beginning. It didn't help that breastfeeding was an excruciating pain that was worse than childbirth, at least for me. My nipples were constantly bleeding. I'm pretty sure Hartford has a pinch of vampire in her because she got used to drinking bloody milk for a while. If you need to go throw up right now, that's fine . . . come back when you're done.

Okay, welcome back.

I spent every feed sobbing, and I mean loud, dry-heaving, wailing sobs. Beau had to hold me as I breastfed, it hurt that bad. We were like those Russian nesting dolls, me holding Hartford, Beau holding me. It got to the point where I had to use nipple shields while I breastfed, which made the milk come out even less. I mean, it's a shield! Because I was constantly trying to get my supply up, I spent most of my day pumping. Pumping is where my loneliness really began. Instead of waking up in the morning and running to kiss and hold my baby, I had to sit for twenty minutes alone in bed, half naked with my weird swollen Jabba the Hutt body hooked up to a machine. Did I feel like a powerful earth goddess mother? Hell no. I felt like a bloated Lord Voldemort.

I hated having to leave the people I was around to sit alone and pump. I hated having to put my baby down to sit alone and pump. I hated having to wake up in the middle of the night to sit alone and pump. There was also this weird psychological aspect to my lack of milk supply. All I kept thinking was that if I had been born in another time period, in the jungle in 1564 or something, I wouldn't have been able to feed my baby enough to keep her alive. I know that probably sounds INSANE, but the thought of that consumed me and made me feel like a failure. I had roman-ticized breastfeeding for so long. I wanted to feel like I was a part of something that had been going on since the beginning of time. I blame all the period pieces that I watch. I love feeling connected to history and like I'm a part of this long line of women who came before me. I wanted to be a part of that breastfeeding womanhood club, and I just couldn't.

I remember the last time I breastfed Hartford after three months of trying to make it work. I cried the whole time because I felt like a failure, and I was saying goodbye to the idea of having that extra connection and closeness with my baby that breastfeeding brings. When it came to being able to do this totally natural thing that mothers had been doing for centuries, I was definitely not girlbossing. I pumped less and less for a week straight until my milk dried out. It took me a while to mourn the death of "what could've been" as a breastfeeding mom. I felt this ever-present feeling of sadness. I grew up imagining what life would be like as a mom, and I always imagined that special closeness with my baby from breastfeeding. If we're not feeling pressure to be a girlboss, then we're feeling pressure to be supermom. It's exhausting!

Metaphorically speaking, I had to go to my own Stassi the Breastfeeding Mom funeral, say my goodbyes, and bury that version of myself. But once I accepted it, I felt so much freer, and more like myself. I wasn't Hartford's or the pump's hostage anymore. I mean, I'm always Hartford's hostage, and now I'm Messer's hostage too, but it was like I got a little bit of slack. I woke up and had free will! It was 100 percent the right choice for me, because after going through all that, I very strongly believe that my mental health and happiness is more important than breast milk. My kids will benefit more from a happy mom. I am fully aware that the "breast is best" contingent hates me right now. Y'all need to relax.

Sometimes I feel guilty even saying out loud that I felt lonely during that time, because Beau was there with me every step of the way, doing 50 percent of the work. It's not that I felt lonely like I had no one to talk to though. I was so thankful to be in the thick of it with him, so thankful I had chosen him to be my partner in this.

It was a loneliness I felt from watching everyone begin to resume their normal lives once the Covid restrictions were lifted. You might think the loneliness came from being isolated *because* of the Covid restrictions, but it was actually the other way around. Giving birth during Covid allowed me to have those first few months postpartum privately and quietly with my baby without feeling the pressure to be doing or accomplishing something. It made me feel better to know we were all at home, like I wasn't missing out on things. But once the world opened up again, I saw everyone resume their old routines and lives. I watched my old cast members start filming the next season of *Vanderpump Rules*, and it stung. I would see Lala's birthday or an event about Katie's sandwich shop and feel like I should have been there. I was at home, hating my new body, my greasy unwashed hair, my sweats, watching my peers start filming the show I had loved so much. I felt like I had to mourn the loss of my career all over again. Mourn the loss of the old me, mourn the loss of my old life.

I also just want to note that two things can be true at once. While I felt seriously lonely and down, I still was so incredibly thankful and happy to have my baby. When I look back on those postpartum months, the joy definitely outweighs the sadness, but it doesn't mean the sadness didn't leave a mark. It was the most complex period of my life, to have so many different conflicting emotions bubbling all at once.

Mourning the loss of your former self is such an under-discussed topic. Even though I welcomed all the changes that came with having babies with open arms, it was still hard to digest that things would literally never be the same again. You will never wake up and live the day for yourself ever again EVER. Even if you go on vacation without your children, there won't be a day that goes by that you don't miss them and think about them and worry about them. Yes, some people are able to maintain some of the life they had pre-children, but for the most part, your day-to-day drastically changes forever. Your priorities, the things you value, the way you like to spend your time. This all even trickles down to the types of hobbies you engage in or the kinds of clothes you buy. I rarely buy skirts or casual dresses anymore, because I know I'm going to be spending most of the day on the floor in the crisscross-applesauce position with my kids, and I don't want to flash everyone. I still like to reminisce about what my life was like before, the places I used to frequent, what my routine used to be, the high heels I wore on a daily basis (RIP).

It wasn't until my sister came to visit, two MONTHS after Hartford was born, that I emerged from my house/cocoon and joined the outside world again. Two months of no sunshine on my face, two months of living like Dracula. I swear my eyes started burning the first time I left the house. I was Lestat from *Interview with the Vampire* going to have cocktails at the Grove. At least I felt more confident because I finally had my hair highlights redone, which breathed new life into my soul. It also helped that my sister always makes me feel great about myself. She's one of my biggest cheerleaders. The second she walked through my front door, she started helping me with Hartford and said all the right things to make me feel like I was a cool mom (I'm not). So even though I could only fit into my maternity leggings and an oversize coat, I had fresh highlights and a sunnier attitude, and we ventured out to the Grove.

Beau and I have been frequenting this restaurant La Piazza at the Grove since the beginning of our relationship. It's one of our favorite places. I've been going there since before I moved to LA. My grandma used to take me when I would visit her, and I've been loyal to it ever since. Not to brag, but I have a drink named after me there. The Sainte Stassi. It's a vodka, St-Germain, prosecco, strawberry martini and it's amazing. It used to be called something else, but I was so committed to them that the owners changed the name. I missed those cocktails so much when I was pregnant, so obviously it was the first place I went once I was ready to leave the house. Needless to say, with both Beau and my sister there to watch Hartford, I had quite a few Sainte Stassis. Before y'all come for me, I pumped and dumped afterward, since I was still in breastfeeding hell.

To be honest, the *best* part about postpartum life (besides having a baby, duh) was the lack of girlbossing. The thought of girlbossing repulsed me, since I was just trying to sit down for a few seconds at a time. That was my main goal. I will say, when I was nine months pregnant with Messer, less than a month away from my due date, I was so ridiculously excited to girlchill. When I had Hartford, I started *Sex and the City* over from the very beginning and spent those first few weeks with my baby cuddled up on the couch. I feel like those first few weeks after you give birth are some of the only times in society where it's socially acceptable to do nothing but girlchill. A few weeks isn't nearly enough time though. Someone please call Elle Woods and tell her to pass some new post-partum legislation.

Real talk, I thought a lot about what it would have been like to be filmed for the show postpartum. Production started filming within days of Scheana Shay giving birth to her daughter, Summer Moon, and I remember seeing all the photos of her out filming for *Vanderpump Rules*—I was in awe. Scheana and I have always had a tumultuous relationship, but when it comes down to it, I will always care about her. I have to give her MAD PROPS for being able to handle that. My blood actually boiled for her that she couldn't spend her first weeks and months having some downtime with her baby. I absolutely would not have been able to film right away. I would've begged production to start later, and if they had told me no, I would've just missed the first few weeks, because I would not have been able to film in all my swollen glory. That would've been a horrible season for me, had I been in that position. There's no way I could've done my job properly. I would've had meltdowns every day . . . which, I guess, wouldn't have been that much different than previous seasons.

Now, you might think, *Oh, meltdowns, that would've made for great TV*. I'm not talking drunken birthday party "fun" melt-downs. I mean sad, depressing, greasy hair I-just-want-to-be-alone-with-my-baby meltdowns. That shit's not entertaining, it's just pitiful. When you're on a show like *Vanderpump Rules*, there is a huge emphasis on looking the best you can. Why do you think we all looked like we were heading to a VIP club in every one-on-one interview? There's also a huge emphasis on nightlife. I genuinely wouldn't have been able to integrate myself into that atmosphere right after I gave birth. I feel like in some of the scenes with Scheana, you can see it on her face. She looked amazing and beautiful, but you could see that she was struggling a bit. Lala also had her daughter a couple of months before filming started, and I remember feeling so frustrated for them when trolls would leave comments mom-shaming them for not being at home with their babies.

It's a job, a career, a way to make a living and support oneself. I'm sure Lala and Scheana would've loved to be at home with their babies, but they have to support themselves *and* their babies. Do other working moms get shamed when they have to go to work? Yes, and no. We're shamed if we do, shamed if we don't. I've had some friends tell me stories about people criticizing them for taking too much maternity leave, and others for taking too little. I think both Lala and Scheana deserve a lot of credit for working during their first postpartum days. I'm not going to say I was relieved to be fired AT ALL, but I was relieved I could go through all the ups and downs that postpartum life brought in private, just Russian nesting dolling with my baby and husband. I wouldn't have been strong enough to handle that on camera and in public.

My biggest takeaway from postpartum life was that I *could* have it all, but not all at the same time. It made me realize that "having it all" was nearly impossible and extremely overrated. I became very satisfied with having just enough. Yes, I was struggling a bit with my mental health, but I was so grateful and happy just being a mom. That was enough for me. We don't need to be having it all, all the time. There's a beauty in that, because when everything is happening for you all at once, it's hard to soak those things up individually and really appreciate each thing independently. But when you're going through any especially active phase in your life, whether it's new motherhood, buying a house, a job promotion, or an epic girls' trip you'd spent over a year planning—that's when you really cherish what you have in the moment. So why would anyone even *want* to have it all at the same time? That sounds exhausting.

Right now, I'm in my "mom era," and because of that, some things need to be put on the back burner. I'm not going to have the best social life right now, I'm not going to be having fun girls' trips on a whim right now. But I am more than fine having just enough with my mom era, because I know that everything in life is temporary and there will come a day when my kids don't need me as much and I'll enter a different era. Maybe the "Both my kids are in school, therefore I'm somewhat free" era, or the "Back in my pre-baby jeans after many, many months" era. Mainly I'm aiming for the "I'm totally chill and happy with everything I have" era. Wish me luck.

Takeaway

It should be socially acceptable and totally normal to mourn the loss of your former self, whether it's going from single to married with kids, from somewhat carefree college student to person with bills and a real job, or human who used to girlboss her way from the office to the club but who now just wants to chill. There should be rituals to mark these "losses" and celebrate the new version of yourself. Why is this not a thing?

CHAPTER 4

Anyone Can "Have It All" . . . with the Right Filter

I don't know about you, but I'm starting to feel like everyone and their sister online owns a Birkin bag, flies on private jets, and takes about seven European vacations a year. It also looks like they eat pasta for every meal while simultaneously fitting into sample-size clothing. Their children never terrorize them, and their homes look like an *Architectural Digest* spread. Am I missing something here? Was I asleep on the day that we all collectively decided to spend over ten grand on a designer bag? And how, I mean, *how*, are people taking so many fancy vacations ALL THE TIME?! Or maybe my algorithm is set to a "make Stassi insecure" setting. It's really hard to watch so many people on social media live what looks like a dream life. They look like they have it all. How do they all have access to a yacht?! And they make it seem so easy to have—

and balance—it all. As much as I talk about being happy with what you have and finding joy in small things, these glimpses of "having it all" are bound to affect you every now and then.

We all know that nothing about social media is truly real (you do know this, right?). And that's okay. If we keep that in mind while we're scrolling, hopefully the "perfect" lives some of these people lead will feel like a fictional movie instead of a documentary. Whenever I get caught up in someone's Instagram account and I start feeling bad about the chaos of my own life, I just gently remind myself that social media is like a Pinterest board. It's curated; it's inspo; it's there to help me come up with ways to romanticize my own life or find great shoes. It's Disney, not PBS. Yes, there are those few accounts that focus on the realness of life, and I love them for showing the messiness and the middle-of-the-night meltdowns (both baby and parent). I am not that bold. You don't see me uploading unflattering photos of myself to my Shutterfly scrapbook or framing photos of myself with the kids where I look like a troll, so why would I do that on social media? Nope, those get deleted. I absolutely do not fault anyone for posting only the picture-perfect moments of their lives. It's not their responsibility to keep my mental health in check—it's mine.

If I showed the real shit, I would be posting Instagram Reels or TikToks of car rides where both children are screaming the entire time. Sometimes Beau and I just look at each other in the car, like, *What horrible things did we do in a past life to get here in this moment?* I always say the soundtrack of our lives is not Beyoncé, it's Hartford's guttural screeching temper-tantrum screams. And if people saw what it took sometimes for me to get a decent OOTD photo? The behind-the-scenes truth would be an hour of me on the verge of tears trying on multiple things that won't fit, even after I've stuffed myself into my postpartum Spanx. Every cute photo of Hartford at a restaurant or Universal Studios or a party should come with a warning that in reality, it took us forty-three minutes to get her out of there to the point where Beau had to take her and (gently) throw her over his shoulder as she screamed. There would be photos of me crying in the nursery rocking chair because Messer is overtired and hasn't stopped crying for hours. Is crying contagious? It might be. It would be photos of my post-baby loose skin. Maybe you'd get lucky and see an Instagram Story showing me and Beau in bed after we put down the kids, literally not talking and just separately scrolling on our phones because we're too exhausted to interact with each other after a long day of parenting. But why would I do that to you?

I love watching a woman open up about the struggles of getting her baby to sleep through the night just as much as I love scrolling through someone's curated feed showing them traipsing around European beaches with zero cellulite and not a care in the world—except maybe what their afternoon cocktail will be. These two things can be true, right? That I love the mess and the perfection? One is relatable and makes me feel like it's not just me who is losing it daily, and the other is like a mindless escape into fantasyland. I love TikTok because once I'm finished seeing everyone's picture-perfect lives on Instagram, I can pop over to TikTok and connect with women on some real shit. Women talking about their crippling post-Covid social anxiety, or a video of a woman hiding in her car in front of her house with her Starbucks coffee for an entire fifteen minutes so she can get some alone time before going inside to her partner and kids. Fifteen minutes of alone time is an eternity for a parent.

I always feel guilty when someone sends me a message asking how Hartford is so perfectly behaved all the time. She's not! She's demonic for at least 36 percent of the day, but the last thing I think about doing when she's having an epic tantrum is whipping out my phone to film it and post it to social media. In those moments, I'm just trying to survive and help my kid work through it. So it gets hard to show the messy stuff. Beau and I have tried everything when it comes to dealing with tantrums. We've seen all the "gentle parenting" tips, we've tried calmly talking her through a meltdown. Spoiler alert: she's incapable of listening to me calmly explain that I understand she has big feelings in my most Ms. Rachel voice when she is in the middle of a tantrum. It infuriates me when people tell me I should serenely lower my voice and communicate with her, saying I understand she's sad that she can't have the remote control and how can we come to a compromise that will satisfy us both. She still believes in the Easter Bunny! There is no rational communication happening. Whose kids are able to pay attention and listen during a tantrum? Mine sure as hell doesn't.

We've tried threatening to take toys away. We've tried bribing her with ice cream, lollipops, even gifts (I know, shameful). We've tried time-out. We've tried yelling, which I didn't ever want to do, I just lose my mind sometimes, and yes, I feel guilty about it. I've even broken down and cried in front of her! To be honest, it worked. She saw me crying and all of a sudden just stopped screaming, but I realized that I couldn't make a habit out of emotionally manipulating my child. We're to the point where the only thing we do now is ignore it. I literally try to ignore her, and trust that she will eventually work through it on her own. I've been around family and friends who have seen me ignore her tantrums, and I feel like they must think I'm straight-up crazy or neglectful. But it's the best way I know how to parent. I just do my best to not match her energy, and to let her work through her own shit. I encourage her to go to her room for some alone time, and most of the time that helps her calm down. Obviously we always still make sure she is safe when she is in that state. I'll either ignore her from the same room or watch on the monitor. But letting her work through her tantrums is the best I can do.

I would like to think I have a well-rounded social media presence, but it does get tricky to be candid when there are so many people eager to pick me apart. I've always prided myself on being someone who tries to be as honest as possible, and I've always said that transparency has been the secret sauce to any success I've ever had in my career. I've talked about my underboob sweat, my relationship insecurities, my chin implant. But the more people who follow me, the more people dissect everything I post. For example, not long after Messer was born, we took him and Hartford out of the house for the first time since I gave birth. We went to lunch at a restaurant we love called the Belmont. I felt comfortable taking them there because our friends are the owners. I knew we'd have a corner booth to sit in, and that I would feel safe there. I posted some photos from the outing and captioned it "Three of us are wearing diapers." I wanted to be honest about the state I was in, while also cracking a little joke. I wish more women talked about how we have to wear diapers for weeks after giving birth. But of course the mom-shamers came for me, and I received countless comments about how:

1. Hartford should be potty trained by now [she was two and a half at the time].

2. I should be breastfeeding. There was a baby bottle and a margarita in one of the photos, so naturally, many people gave their "breast is best" opinions.

3. I was "putting my baby in danger" by taking him out in public at ten days old. Never mind the fact that I held him the whole time. You would've thought I was passing him around to everyone at the restaurant, giving him tequila shots, and feeding him spicy buffalo wings with the way people were commenting about me taking my baby out in public.

When I try to be honest (I'm wearing diapers), people pick it apart and shame me for it (you're wearing diapers!). It turns into a debate in the comment section that ultimately makes me feel bad about myself. It makes it harder to be open and real. We say we want honesty from people on social media, and then a handful of people have to go and spoil that, which only prolongs the problem that everything we see on social media is somewhat fake. It's an annoying cycle we can't get out of. And don't even get me started on clickbait headlines. I talk about this a lot on my podcast. So much of what I post or say gets turned into a headline that is 100 percent taken out of context, to make it seem like it's much more salacious than it is.

Here's an example. I went on Alex Cooper's *Call Her Daddy* podcast when I was pregnant. She asked me about the Ozempic craze that was newly sweeping the world at the time. I was honest and joked about how I had absolutely googled it and wondered about it, and that I was tempted to try it after I gave birth. I mean, come on, if you've heard of Ozempic, and you're someone who has insecurities about your weight, then you cannot tell me you haven't been curious. If you haven't heard of it, it's a diabetes drug that celebrities and tech CEOs and anyone with money who wanted to lose weight fast started taking. Now there are several brands that are solely prescribed to people for weight loss, so it's pretty much old news.

On that podcast, I joked that Ozempic was essentially like taking vitamins. Cut to a trillion headlines reading "Stassi Schroeder says Ozempic is like taking vitamins." A headline like that is a tad misleading. They didn't say "Stassi Schroeder *joked* that Ozempic is like taking vitamins." Instead, it reads like I am spreading false medical information about a weight-loss drug. Not ideal. I thought I was being real, and it got spun into something that makes me sound like a complete asshole. And then there are the people who read the headline without listening to the podcast and actually believe that I'm saying Ozempic is a vitamin, earning me a few more haters. I want to be myself on social media. I want to be open, honest, candid, frank, transparent, *all* the things. But it's getting harder and harder to do that, because sometimes it feels like it's not worth all the aftermath. Sometimes I'd just rather post something pretty and safe so that I can spare myself the shaming in my comment section.

With all of that said, I've found ways to be open and honest about my life while also still trying to protect myself. Firstly, I treat my Instagram page like a photo album I want to look at. For the most part, I don't go posting crazy thoughts or opinions anywhere that has a comment section—or even casual thoughts and opinions. Turns out there are lots of people who get offended by . . . just about everything. I posted a TikTok about how I didn't want my son to be born in August because I thought the month's peridot birthstone was ugly. I mean, lime green isn't my color, what can I say? I went to the comment section of my video, and there were a ridiculous amount of people who were apparently born in August who took major offense to this, as if it were a personal attack on their character and integrity instead of an opinion about jewelry. I had to laugh at how ridiculous it was, but it also solidified my rule of not wanting to post anything polarizing where there is a comment section.

If people want to shame me by sending a private message, that works for me. I can choose not to engage and pretend it doesn't exist. I've also made a little bit of peace with the fact that what I say on my podcast will continue to be taken out of context by gossip sites. I'm not going to filter myself because I'm afraid a tabloid will intentionally misquote me. That's not what I'm about. I'm most open on *The Good the Bad the Baby*, which is the Patreon podcast I share with Beau. To be completely frank, it's behind a paywall, so I know that 99 percent of the people listening aren't people who are out to get me. I mean, you have to be a pretty dedicated and well-off troll to *pay* to hear someone you just want to tear down. So that podcast feels safe, and I'm able to share almost everything there. So if you think my Instagram is painting this "perfect" picture of my kids frolicking in pumpkin patches and singing *Frozen* songs, please understand that I have so many more moments where they are screaming, the house is a mess, and I am barely holding it together. But during those moments, I am way too stressed to start making and posting videos.

And yes, some of my photos are posed and filtered and taken by a professional. I shared pregnancy photos taken in a studio with great lighting, and they make it look like my daughter is an angel (I mean, she is *most* of the time) and that my pregnant belly was a fashion statement. Why? Because I wanted to! Hartford and Messer can look back at those photos and share them with their own kids one day, if they want kids. There's such a stigma around photo editing, and I get the argument that it sets unrealistic beauty standards. Do some people take it a little too far? Maybe. I'll never forget a conversation I had when I was pregnant the first time around. I was talking to an unnamed friend, and she was ripping apart someone else's maternity photos and talking about how photoshopped they were. Hearing her talk about it that way, with so much judgment, weirdly broke my heart a little.

First of all, this friend had never been pregnant before, so she had no idea what pregnancy does to you mentally and emotionally. Watching your body change and become a host for another living being is a mindfuck. It's so out of your control, and it takes a toll on a lot of women, myself included. So what if this pregnant woman wanted to edit her maternity photos as if she were on the cover of *Vanity Fair*? Maybe she wanted to remember her pregnancy a little more fondly than what she was experiencing, which was probably something like a beached whale mixed with a sloth. Maybe she didn't want to remember her body exactly as it was. What is wrong with that? That's her prerogative. And that's every person's right whether they're pregnant or not. If it makes us feel better about ourselves to head to FaceApp and hit "Charm" level 2, then why not? As long as we aren't lying and captioning our photos "zero filter, zero edits!" I don't see the problem. I don't know that I've ever posted a story without swiping once to the "Paris" filter. I assumed that everyone else was doing the same thing.

I got to know a popular influencer via social media, and we ended up hanging out a few times. One night when we went to dinner, she started berating me about my dependence on the Paris filter, and almost bragging about how she doesn't use it. The whole time I just kept thinking, *Why the heck wouldn't you use it? Are you the Joan of Arc of Instagram filters?* Do you really think you're doing something noble here by posting your video as is? Like, *how brave.* I know it doesn't make me deep or qualify me to be a CNN Hero, but I just like the way I look with the Paris filter smoothing some shit out. Needless to say, it was a weird conversation, and it was odd to feel shamed for a little bit of face smoothing.

I might be all for some online filtering or wrinkle-smoothing, but there is also a glorious freedom that comes with accepting that things are never going to be perfect in your life. That doesn't mean I won't use a filter to just make it look a *little* bit shinier. Life is not black and white, but it can be greasy. You can criticize people who present perfection and also love their beautiful children and garden and chef's kitchen that doesn't have a single juice spill or Goldfish crumb in sight even though they have four children. I can be transparent about things in my life but also choose not to show my children in an epic tantrum. A little Paris filter never hurt anyone, right?

I don't think people still say this, but . . . YOLO. You really do only live once, so you may as well not spend it stressing about trying to reach perfection in every aspect of your life. I have perfectionist tendencies, which I have to watch out for. There are moments in life when I just decide to let go of things and embrace the chaos of whatever is happening, and my day becomes so much better than it would have been if I'd worried about a messy living room or baby food in my hair. When Messer was born, that panic hit hard and fast. I would look around my living room that I had meticulously decorated and see it cluttered not just with Hartford's toys but with baby toys and bottles and blankets and snot rags covering every once-chic surface. Suddenly there was a makeshift diaper-changing station, a bassinet, leftover macaroni noodles from who knows how many meals ago, broken crayons, stickers all over my pretty coffee table, Hartford's underwear hanging off my decorative crystal obelisk. The list goes on.

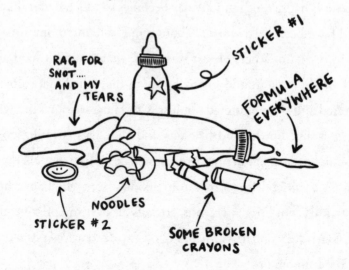

RIP TO MY CHIC OBELISK

Whenever I saw *other* people's homes on social media, it seemed like everything was spotless all the time, like their children despised toys or had read and absorbed the kiddie version of Marie Kondo or something. Then one day while I was taking my stress out on Beau, I looked around and realized that one day our kids will be grown and I'll be longing for the mess. With that one thought, I was able to embrace the chaos and the fact that my living room wasn't perfect anymore. That thought took the pressure off, and I started to enjoy my days so much more. I felt a little freer, and a lot lighter, even if my obelisk was hidden under a pile of laundry.

MOM DECOR

RAG FOR SNOT.... AND MY TEARS

STICKER #1

FORMULA EVERYWHERE

STICKER #2

NOODLES

SOME BROKEN CRAYONS

I know it's way freaking easier said than done, but I found that in order for me to accept that things will never be perfect, I had to learn the art of not giving a shit. Now, obviously this is impossible to a certain extent. I'm not a superhero or a complete monster. I obviously do care about what people think of me and my home, but I've had to learn to care less. I still have moments where I worry about whether my house is nice enough to have a party, or whether someone I look up to will think my outfits are chic enough. I worry that the other moms at Hartford's school will judge me for the fact that Beau drops her off at school and not me. I mean, I had a newborn to take care of every morning. Despite all my worry, I really do make an effort to practice not giving a shit. I make an effort to talk myself out of those feelings, and I refuse to let them take up too much space in my head. When I see negative comments now, it doesn't sting as much as it used to. All of that takes practice though.

The art of not giving a shit really comes in handy when I'm dealing with my kids. Most people assume my daughter is a little angel, but as I've mentioned before, she can be terrifying. She fully Dark Passengers. If you don't know what I'm talking about, here's the deal: When I was on *Vanderpump Rules*, Beau started referring to my mammoth-size emotional meltdowns as the Dark Passenger. I wrote about this in my last book, and I've talked a lot about it on my podcast. The Dark Passenger describes the exact moment that I get so angry and activated that I start seeing red, and there is no talking me down from my rage. I haven't Dark Passenger–ed in years (well, not fully), and I always assumed that I used to Dark Passenger because trust issues and alcohol don't mix, but Hartford is sober, y'all, and she's had zero time to develop trust issues, so as it turns out, it's genetic and can be passed down. What can I say, it's in my DNA.

Not only does Hartford Dark Passenger in the privacy of our home, she's also very keen on doing it in public. If you were to see me in a grocery store parking lot trying to get her into her car seat, you would think I was kidnapping someone's child. You would legit look over and say, "Is that Stassi Schroeder? Why is she kidnapping a child?" And I'm not joking when I say there have been plenty of mornings where I've had to play hype music while I'm getting ready and doing my makeup, just so I have the courage to bring her out of the house by myself. We never know when she's going to have an epic Dark Passenger tantrum. It's not safe anywhere. This gets extra terrifying for me because people will recognize me when we go out. One of my worst fears is that I'll see some tip on a gossip account about how I couldn't handle my kids and they were melting down at the Grove or wherever, and that I must be a shitty mom.

There was a TikTok that went viral about an Uber Eats delivery person and Kylie Jenner. An Uber Eats guy had delivered food to Kylie Jenner's house, and he made a TikTok about how he could hear her baby crying, implying that Kylie Jenner was a shitty parent. First of all, that invasion of her privacy is diabolical. Secondly, babies cry. That's what they do, like, A LOT of the time. I couldn't believe that people started commenting that she must be an absent mother because her baby was crying. For a while, because I was so scared of someone judging the way I parented Hartford during one of her meltdowns, I actually started leaving the house less. If Beau couldn't come with us somewhere, I would just stay home with Hartford. That's insane and also not fair to my daughter. So I had to think, *Okay, what's the worst that could happen? So what if someone makes a TikTok about Hartford melting down? Is it the end of the world?* I know I'm doing the absolute best I can. I may not always nail it, but I really try hard. If someone judges me, I have to do my best to let that go.

I remember the first time I took Hartford to the Grove alone after I had that epiphany. She loves to play in the little water fountain statues scattered around the outdoor mall, and when I told her we had to go home, her meltdown was monumental. Once again I looked like I was kidnapping her. She did indeed Dark Passenger. But something else happened. As this was all going down, I had multiple people coming up to me and sympathizing. They were all saying, "I'm so sorry, I've been there, girl." I felt like I was part of that mom club, the one full of women who have really seen some shit. Because of that support, I realized that if for some reason something went viral online about Hartford melting down in public, at least there would be a lot of women out there who could relate and maybe then feel less alone with their own tiny Dark Passengers. When you learn not to give a shit, it normally all works out, and you have a better time. I'm telling you, letting go of the pressure to be perfect and not giving a shit does wonders for the soul.

Most of our moms didn't have to add social media pressures to their list of things that stressed them out. They had worries, but they didn't have to imagine those worries winding up on Twitter or X or Instagram or Threads or whatever social media platforms have gone in and out of fashion by the time you read this. I asked my mom what it was like for her, back when all you showed your friends were the actual photos you had developed and then put into an actual photo album or frame. I asked if she felt pressure from other moms, but I knew what her answer would be before she opened her mouth.

My mom was an IDGAF-what-others-think-about-me type of mom. I always admired that she lived her life the way *she* wanted. She was the quintessential divorced hot mom: confident, always put together, unafraid to wear leather pants and crop tops. The only time she felt insecure and like she was being mom-shamed or didn't have her shit together was at the Los Angeles Country Club—big surprise. Feeling insecure at a country club! My paternal grandparents were members, and some of my greatest memories with them are at the LA Country Club. I'm from New Orleans, but my grandparents had a home in Los Angeles, and I lived the first few years of my life there. In LA, not the club. When my mom married my dad and had me and my brother, dinners and lunches at the country club were a very regular thing. My mom said that every other mom had her kids in matching monogrammed outfits, and they were always so well-behaved, as if they were lobotomized Stepford toddlers. Those Chanel-clad moms loved to discuss all the different structured activities their children were in—piano, ballet, theater, chess, etiquette classes. The country club was my mom's version of a social media comment thread. But at least she got breaks from the shaming when she went home. We live with social media mom-shaming 24-7, but I know that's a choice. We could log off any time, but then how would we know how to make the viral baked feta pasta or learn to use a Dyson Airwrap?

After everything you've just read about me trying to let go of perfection, I actually love momfluencers. Hear me out. Some of them serve as major inspo for me. I think of them the same way I do romantic comedies. They're a fantasy, and a source of fun, lighthearted entertainment. It's all feel-good vibes. I even think the momfluencers (some of them) would be the first to tell you that their lives are just as chaotic as yours or mine. They're curating an image for us to enjoy and take inspiration from—and, yes, they're usually selling something. I know it's easy to feel bad about the chaos of our own lives when we see such perfectly curated accounts, but once you accept the fact that it isn't real and it's a form of entertainment, it's much more fun to just take in the image they're presenting and maybe get some ideas for how to decorate a nursery or pick the right nonstick pan to cook with instead of hating on them.

One of my favorite accounts to follow is @ballerinafarm. As I write this, this mother, Hannah, is pregnant with her eighth child, and they literally farm and live off the land. She makes these impressive homemade meals *every single day*. I'm talking sourdough pancakes, grilled lavender honey peaches with homemade vanilla custard, everything-from-scratch lasagna. And I mean EVERY-THING is from scratch. I think she makes her own sourdough bread daily. I am not joking. And it's not just that; she always has multiple children crawling all over her in her videos, yet she always looks gorgeous and calm. I mean, SEVEN kids with one on the way?! I'm sure she has a few nannies helping her out behind the scenes, and I definitely did a stalkery deep dive and discovered that her husband's family is incredibly wealthy, and his father was the founder of JetBlue. Knowing those details made me feel so much better about why I sometimes struggle to make HelloFresh dinners, which are like a paint-by-numbers form of cooking. The point is, we don't always know what someone's backstory is. We don't know how much effort or help went into making a certain video or post. So I've made a choice to look at these accounts as entertainment and inspo, not as a documentary that I should be comparing my life to.

If we were inundated with nothing but the hard parts of parenting, we'd probably stop procreating immediately. Yes, I like seeing women keep it real on social media and talk about the struggles of motherhood, but I want to see the fake, fluffy stuff too. Show me homemade lavender pancakes and an adorable farmstead with precious children devoid of snot or rage any day. It's easy to get caught up in how hard parenting can be, so maybe looking at a beautiful mom in a flowy dress with her children each delicately picking eggs out of their sustainable chicken coop is a healthy distraction. As long as we don't start thinking something is missing in our own lives, and remember that behind the scenes and when the camera is off, at least one of those children is going to have an epic, colossal meltdown, and someone, probably the mom, will have to wipe their snot.

To: Social Media
From: Stassi
(really everyone)

Dear Social Media,

It's been fifteen years since we first met (almost twenty if we're counting MySpace). I don't know if I've said this enough, but I've cherished so much of the time we've spent together. Yes, it's been a roller coaster of emotions, but every meaningful relationship comes with highs and lows. If we didn't experience the lows together, then how would we really appreciate the highs? Not only have you inspired me in so many ways (I love your Parisian-style interior design photos) but you've also made me laugh like no one else has ever done before (I literally LOL'd at all those Pedro Pascal memes). You've helped me grow into the woman I am today, and you've taught me so much about life. I now know the human race is so ridiculous that people can turn into feral animals over insulated travel mugs.

If it weren't for you, I would never have discovered sixty-second history TikToks on how the Victorians used to make candles, realized my affinity for coastal gran culture, or learned how to contour my face with self-tanner. You informed me that skinny jeans were out and taught me what a beige flag is. And *during the dark times of 2020, you provided me with endless posts about funfetti baking hacks. You kept me company when I needed it the most and have been the only one I could rely on to be there for me at any hour of the day, besides my husband. You were there for every 3:00 a.m. feeding with my babies, and every moment I had to spend in the waiting room of a doctor's appointment. For that I am forever grateful.*

With that said, we've also been through some rough patches, but what relationship hasn't? I've posted some truly cringeworthy things, and I'll live with that shame forever. And while you've connected me with so many wonderful people, you've also exposed me to quite a few scary ones, like @user9823729384089, or Linda, mother of six (three of them doggies), proud wife, favorite Bible verse Matthew 5:16. There have also been plenty of times where I felt you were mildly abusive. Thank you for acknowledging that and creating the "Restrict" option for me. I want to be completely transparent and honest here (something you should work harder on), and admit that our relationship has been a tad toxic at times, but I think we've worked through that. Yes, you've made me feel like I wasn't good enough, and you've definitely gaslit me into thinking I was always the problem, but you made up for that by providing me with the most perfectly tailored TikTok algorithm and by helping me pay my bills (sponcon FTW). I guess we're both maturing and learning to grow together. I've come to terms with the fact that you're kind of phony and fake as sh*t. I accept you for you.

What I'm trying to say is this: After every break we've taken, we still always find our way back to each other, and that has to mean something. Despite it all, Social Media, I think I still love you.

xx Stassi

P.S. Could you do me a favor and take the "Seen" feature off my read direct messages on Instagram? thx ♥

Takeaway

Yes, social media sometimes crushes people's self-esteem, and it hasn't been the best for teen girls if you read one of the eight million articles about the topic. Still. It's here, it helps us find good recipes or inspirational people or homes, and sometimes it's funny. It can also be toxic, but remembering to let go of the pressure to be perfect and not give a damn does wonders for the soul. Use your favorite filter, but remember that social media is not a documentary, and those glossy, perfect lives you're seeing are probably just as messy as yours when the camera is off.

CHAPTER 5

Warning: Girlbossing While Pregnant Is Bad for Your Mental Health

The hours, weeks, and months after giving birth can be tough. *But* you also have permission to lie on the couch and watch TV because you have a vagina or a C-section scar to heal! With Hartford I had no clue what to expect, but the second time around I was seriously looking forward to the first few weeks postpartum. Obviously I was excited because my baby would be here, but *also* because of all the downtime. With my second pregnancy, I planned ahead.

I spent weeks deciding what to watch. Should I rewatch *Medici* on Netflix, or try something new? I even asked my podcast listeners for recommendations and ultimately decided I needed autumn vibes, since the baby was due in early fall. I wanted to light my pumpkin pecan waffle candles and feel cozy, even though it was still ninety degrees outside. I wanted to drink the new Starbucks autumnal coffee flavor. I wanted to pretend I was living in New England somewhere and the leaves were falling. Because of this, I ultimately decided on *Gilmore Girls*, which I had never seen before. It takes place in a cozy New England town called Stars Hollow, which has total fall vibes. After bingeing it for weeks, I seriously wondered what the hell I was doing in high school when everyone else was watching this truly iconic, amazing show. Best decision ever. Hartford even started watching it with me, and we would sing the theme song together. My whole family was totally immersed in Stars Hollow for a month of our lives, and it was glorious.

With my first pregnancy, I had no idea what I was in for, so the second time around, I wanted to prioritize my mental health. I wanted to make every attempt possible to look chic and somewhat attractive in the hospital, because when I feel like I look good, my mood is a million times better and I'm way more pleasant to be around. Yes, this might sound aggressive since I'm writing a book about taking the pressure off ourselves, but what can I say, I like to feel chic. When I was in the hospital with Hartford, I felt so truly disgusting. I was swollen and greasy and wore this black breastfeeding-friendly tank top and an ill-fitting cotton robe from Amazon most days. Not even a monogram could have made this robe cute. I was going to do my best to help myself *not* feel like a beached whale/sloth this time around. I thought about the things that made me feel good, whether I'm swollen and puffy or not. The obvious answer was jewelry. Yes, people, I packed a jewelry box to take for my son's birth.

FANCY YET FUNCTIONAL

I wanted to feel like freaking Elizabeth Taylor in that hospital. I wanted Messer's first impressions of the world to be of gold and diamonds. Then I thought about clothes that would make me feel chic even though my ankles might be the width of semitruck tires. The answer? Button-downs. I always feel chic in an oversize button-down, so I chose a beautiful light blue oversize poplin button-down shirt dress from Skims, and it truly was a game changer. Goodbye, dreary black robe. Hello, Pregnant Stassi 2.0 in a blue chic button-down. I also made sure to pack my makeup bag so I could feel a little less like Gollum than I had the last time. And finally, because I love a theme, and a spicy skinny margarita was what I was truly looking forward to as my first post-birth treat (per usual), I brought fluffy slippers that had a bedazzled margarita and tequila bottle on them. Y'all may laugh at what I packed in my hospital bag, but let me tell you, my mood was a million times better because I felt cute. Seriously, pack some slippers with a bedazzled anything on them in your hospital bag and thank me later.

ON-BRAND COZY SLIPPERS

Real talk, everything about my second pregnancy was different. Before we conceived Messer,

I was genuinely so afraid to be pregnant again, because I associated pregnancy with being under house arrest. Even though I knew I wanted another baby, I spent a pretty decent amount of time pushing it off because my pregnancy experience with Hartford in 2020 was obviously not the best. Like I've said, I had gotten fired from my jobs, couldn't leave my house, and I spent the majority of my time baking and eating funfetti cakes resulting in nearly sixty-five pounds of weight gain. My relationship to funfetti cake might be the most complex relationship I've ever had. I had to actively force myself to not think about its sugary deliciousness this time around, as if funfetti were some toxic fuckboy. Every time Hartford wanted me to bake cupcakes with her when I was pregnant, I would have to take them to the park so she could share them with friends, otherwise I wouldn't have been able to stop myself. I am truly in awe of people who are able to consume just one funfetti cupcake and feel like that's enough. That's a superpower in my eyes. Funfetti and I are like a divorced couple who every six months have a drunken hookup in between other relationships. Log cakes, on the other hand. That's my Christmas vice, and I will never give them up.

While I was worrying about being pregnant again, I did a *Straight Up with Stassi* podcast episode with Jackie Oshry, one of the hosts of *The Toast* podcast, which changed my outlook. She had also been pregnant during the pandemic, and we were talking about the possibility of having more children. I told her all about my pregnancy worries, like my fear of being stuck at home under a pile of baked goods, and she said she felt the opposite way. She was excited to get pregnant again, since this time she knew she would be able to have more of a life since she could leave her prison cell/house and go into the world. She'd be able to put together cute maternity OOTDs, and maybe even travel. When I heard her explain it like that, I realized I had been looking at it all wrong. Instead of fearing my second pregnancy because of my past, I started to look forward to it and view it as an opportunity to have a completely different experience this time around.

I vowed that if I was lucky enough to get pregnant again, I would make every effort to do it differently this time around. Meaning, instead of lounging around with zero jobs, I would do *all the jobs*, and take very little time off. I planned a national podcast tour while I was pregnant, because that's pretty much the opposite of being stuck at home jobless. I hired a trainer to help get me in shape, because I really wanted to be one of those fashionable pregnant ladies who can just throw on a head-to-toe spandex number and look chic. I avoided my couch (for the most part) and the baking aisle at the grocery store. I even went to some events and did a magazine shoot, which involved me actually getting glammed up. I kept myself busy . . . until I burned out. I realized I was coming dangerously close to girlbossing again, this time while pregnant, and I needed to chill out.

I had been embracing this whole anti-girlboss, "you can't have it all," "take the pressure off" theme for the past few years. But the second I got pregnant again, I rejected it, and it fully backfired. I was able to maintain this go-go-go life until my last podcast show, which fell on my thirty-fifth birthday in Los Angeles, when I was twenty-seven weeks pregnant. I made a commitment to the tour, so I felt like I had to follow through. The second it was finished, though, I got sick, I was exhausted, I crashed. I did one vitamin-infusion IV on tour, but I don't think it really helped. It takes an act of god to give a pregnant woman in her third trimester energy. I never made another appointment with my trainer again, and I waddle-sprinted straight to the couch. I was also starting to feel bouts of sadness because it wasn't just going to be me, Beau, and Hartford anymore. Life as we had known it was going to change, again. And then I got mad at myself for pushing myself to do so much, when what I really wanted was to just relax, sit down, and spend time with my daughter while she was still my only child. I spent the last two and a half months of my pregnancy allowing myself to just be chill. Girlbossing too much just doesn't work for me anymore. I get truly downcast when I haven't seen my kids enough; I get sad when I've spent more time working than I have with them. I now fully understand those movie stars who announce they're taking time off from their career to spend more time with their kids. That's a privilege to be able to do that, but I GET IT.

I girlbossed the shit out of this second pregnancy, and burned myself out. I became resentful that I didn't get to just chill out and cook a baby, even though I actively and intentionally am the one who committed to working so much. I had no one to blame but myself. Learning to ease up and give myself grace is a lesson I'm still learning. But the experience did teach me that it's not worth it to try to do it all. It definitely solidified my opinion that doing too much in some relentless quest for success is not the vibe.

One thing I did not go overboard with was my birth plan. Just like the first time around, my birth plan was no plan, except an epidural and margaritas afterward. I was going to hope for the best and rely on the doctor, because when it comes to childbirth, you cannot control *anything*. I will say I am a fan of castor oil, which is supposed to speed things along. By the end of the third trimester, I don't like being pregnant, and I just want to get the show on the road and get to the rest of my life. (Even if I *did* want to hold my son in until September because that peridot lime-green birthstone is not my thing.) Then Hartford's first day of school was on September 6, and I was determined to make it to her first day, so once we dropped her off that first day I started drinking the castor oil. Looking back, I cannot believe I managed to swallow this stuff, multiple times. It tasted and felt like whale blubber, or how I imagine whale blubber would taste and feel. My hack is to shake it really hard and mix it with orange juice, then down it like a shot. It'll still make you gag, but drinking it plain is straight-up abusive. I'm gagging just thinking about it.

As soon as we picked up Hartford from school I felt crampy, and when the contractions started coming hard and fast—like one minute apart—I started freaking out. I texted Talitha, who is a doula and night nurse, and she told me to get into the shower or bath and she'd be right over. Hartford would not let me get into the shower alone, so I found myself naked in the shower with my daughter watching, leaning into the shower wall with the worst pain I've ever felt. When Hartford started going, "Mommy, open the purple shampoo! No open the green one!" I realized I was in some sort of pregnancy purgatory and I made Beau take Hartford out of the bathroom. Talitha had me do these weird exercise stretchy things. I was basically doing a handstand off the side of my bed yelling, "I'm going to throw up or die!"

When Hartford saw me, she started going, "Mommy crying!" It was terrifying.

Eventually Beau, myself, and Talitha got in the car and sped to the hospital. We left Hartford home alone with some snacks. Just kidding. She was with a responsible adult, I promise. I was in the back of the car gripping the headrest and screaming. As soon as we walked in I growled, "Give me the epidural!" Instead, they asked me to answer a bunch of questions on an iPad like: *Have you done crack over the last nine months? Yes or No.* I finally got the epidural, and they told me I was six centimeters dilated, so I figured I'd have ten hours or so to binge *Gilmore Girls.* I wasn't in Stars Hollow for long before I felt like something was legit trying to get out of my vagina, like an alien was pushing its way out and it was not planning on stopping. I told one of the nurses I thought I was ready to push but she said it was too soon.

"Can you check?" I asked.

"I think you're fine; it's still too soon," she said.

"It really feels like an alien is clawing its way out of my vagina RIGHT NOW. Please check."

So she opened the blanket covering my legs and when she peered in there her face looked shocked. Not the most comforting thing to see.

"I'm going to get the midwife," she said before hurrying off. The midwife came and peered in.

"You have a bulging bag," the midwife said.

Excuse me? What the fuck is a bulging bag?! I asked her this question much more politely, even though I was scared as shit. Who wants a bulging bag in or around their vagina? She said those two words about seventeen times, or maybe it was two or three and it just felt like seventeen times. If you want to know, it's the amniotic sac, which was still intact as my son's head emerged from my vagina since my water hadn't broken yet. So his head was emerging encased in this bag of fluid, kind of like I was giving birth to an alien.

"Can we please stop saying *bulging bag*?" I asked.

The doctor came in to see the bulging bag for himself.

"Okay, push," he said.

I am not lying when I say I pushed for under sixty seconds before a baby slid out. It was so alarmingly fast, Beau and I had zero time to process that we suddenly had a son. The first time we had hours to grasp the reality of what was happening, and the second time there was no buildup at all. It was just like . . . that's a baby. It was so quick that I asked the doctor if I could have possibly laughed the baby out if *Gilmore Girls* had made me giggle before he got there.

"Possibly," he said.

After those contractions I experienced, I feel like I've been through shit, like I've been to war. When you make it through that kind of pain, there is a real "You can't fuck with me now" vibe that comes over you. Before Messer was born, I made sure to bully Beau during our podcast tour so he would not sleep and snack his way through the first few hours of having a crying, helpless infant. After Hartford was born, Beau slept on a chair in the hospital room while I stressed out about how to care for a tiny baby. Like, how were we suddenly responsible for *a human*? He'd then complained about how uncomfortable the chair was!!

The second time around I was like, *Hell no*. All my public shaming paid off, because he took about four Excedrin so he'd stay awake, pledging that he would not sleep, but then the birth was so quick he was wired and couldn't sleep at all. So the second time around, I slept. A little.

After having two kids, I feel like pregnancy is the ultimate "you can't have it all" reminder. If you were getting close to a place in your life where you felt like you might maybe possibly be coming close to having it all, pregnancy swoops in to smack you in the face and shake it out of you. Pregnancy is nothing but a long list of things you can't do, eat, or drink, but it goes deeper than that. You also lose a part of yourself when you go through pregnancy and motherhood. Not to scare the shit out of prospective mothers, but the second you see that positive pregnancy test, so much of who you once were changes. At least it was that way in my experience.

When people say parents shouldn't complain because there are people out there who can't conceive, I understand that, and it's heartbreaking. But if we're telling moms they can't complain or vent, then we're literally telling moms to not feel, and if we do feel, we're told to hide it and pretend everything is perfect. The argument that we should just feel lucky and shut up offers moms who are struggling zero support and ends up making them feel even more alone than they felt before.

Like a psycho, I gave myself two weeks of maternity leave before I started podcasting and writing and doing all the things again. Those two weeks zoomed by, and there I was, sore, exhausted, and . . . working my diaper-clad ass off. Yes, I work from home and make my own schedule and I had a choice to go back (or not) so soon, but the pressure I put on myself to prove I could handle everything was intense. I was telling Talitha, the doula who is also my friend, that I regretted going back so soon and that all I wanted to do was be with my babies, but she said, "Do you really think you'd be happy not doing your podcasts or writing your book, and just staying home with the babies all day?" I had to admit that no, I probably wouldn't be.

I *love* my kids, but I also love the part of me that gets to be an adult and work and create. I would probably lose my mind being a full-time stay-at-home parent. That is the hardest job of all. So once again I realized you just can't win. There is no one single perfect way to do life or parent or work or all three at once. I want to provide for my family and travel and that motivates me to work hard. As much as I want to be a cottagecore soft girl and grow basil while knitting baby bonnets all day, working makes me feel proud of myself. I cannot be with my kids 24-7 *and* work hard, so I have to accept that there will be sacrifices along the way. And if it sounds like I think being a mother is all drudgery and agony, here's the deal . . . To me, this is parenthood in a nutshell: When my kids wake up in the morning is my favorite time of day, and when my kids go to sleep at night is *also* my favorite time of day. I am sure other moms and dads out there get it. IYKYK.

I would definitely not recommend going back to work two weeks after dealing with excruciating contractions and bulging bags. Whether it's childbirth or some other major life event that causes you to need to PULL BACK, do it. Don't rush back just because you think that means you're failing. I had one shot to fully embrace my inner soft girl, and I blew it. Also, no matter how badass you want to be, it's not easy to feel like a boss when you're wearing an adult diaper.

CHAPTER 6

If You Don't Feel Mom Guilt, Are You Actually Even Alive?

oward the end of my 2023 podcast tour, I found myself sprinting—while pregnant—through the Chicago airport. Beau, Taylor, Lo, and I were late and trying to make it onto our flight back home to Los Angeles. It was all very *Home Alone*, except that it was REAL and I just wanted to get home to Hartford, not Macaulay Culkin. We made it to the gate, but it was a packed flight, so they were offering five-hundred-dollar vouchers to people who agreed to take a later plane. My days of being carefree in my early twenties and taking those vouchers are long gone. There was no way I was missing that flight.

The ticket agent scanned my boarding pass. I was ready to shove my pregnant, sweating, swollen self down into a tiny airplane seat and go home.

"Miss?" asked a squinty eyed male gate agent.

"Yes?"

"You're pregnant."

Maybe he was going to sneak me some snacks, or congratulate me for growing a whole human inside my body?

"Thank you?"

"You can't board the plane," he said. "You're seated on an exit row."

"But I can do all the things," I said. I was desperate to get home so I was gonna *be* in that exit row. "I work out! I have a trainer! I can handle this."

"Miss, you need to have a seat until we can get everyone on the plane."

What else was there to do at that point but shed a few fake tears? That got the attention of a nearby female gate agent. She looked at me, with my pretend tears, and said to the guy, "Albert, just let it go."

Thank you, female gate agent who I'll probably never see again! I got on the plane and managed to sit in an exit row without killing anyone or causing the plane to crash into the ocean because clearly pregnant women are incompetent and helpless. It's messed up that pregnancy causes people like Albert to treat you like a walking Fabergé egg. I love a Fabergé egg and *sometimes* it's nice to be treated like one, but not when you're riddled with guilt and you're trying to go home to see your child. I'm proud of myself for working hard, but I'm also terrified that I'm a bad mom for being away. That is basically the definition of mom guilt: doing something that makes you happy, and immediately feeling like the shittiest human and mother on the planet for doing those things.

Once we got onto the plane, Taylor said I should have looked into Albert's beady eyes and said, with a straight face, "I'm not pregnant. What are you talking about? This is how my body looks." I wish I'd said that, but mom guilt is a powerful freaking force. It scrambles your brain and makes you believe things that are *insane.* Like that you're a horrible, selfish parent, when you are probably a totally adequate or even amazing parent. Hartford was having a great time at home with my mom, while I was freaking out that she'd hate me forever if I got home a few hours later than planned. Toddlers don't understand time! To them, yesterday means tomorrow, tomorrow means today, and today is whatever you're doing right that moment. Still, I felt like she had a freaking Swiss timepiece on her tiny wrist and she was counting the seconds until I got home. She definitely was not.

Mom guilt starts before a baby is born, and it probably doesn't stop until we actually die. And even then, it probably stays with us when we're ghosts floating around benevolently haunting our children.

Here's another example. We took Hartford to Universal Studios when I was pregnant with Messer. Her favorite ride is the *Secret Life of Pets* ride, based on the movie. It literally moves about negative twenty miles per hour. It's the slowest fucking ride in the history of amusement park rides. I get in next to Hartford, and

Beau sits in the two-seater car behind us. The ride attendant comes around pulling down the safety bars and she can't get mine down. I guess she couldn't see that I had a giant balloon for a belly, and she kept trying to push it down to the level she was used to on a nonpregnant human. Finally I told her I was pregnant, so she'd stop pushing my stomach.

"Can you please stop pushing the bar down? I'm pregnant. . . ."

Instead of smiling and telling me how wonderful this news was, she gasped, as if I'd just admitted to going on a cross-country killing spree (while pregnant). Everyone looked over at me, trying to see what all the drama was about. Was I really putting my unborn baby in danger? I wasn't smoking a Marlboro Light while hang gliding and chugging a jug of pinot grigio, I was sitting with my daughter on the *Secret Life of Pets* ride. I didn't see any signs saying pregnant women were forbidden, so either the ride employee was a little overzealous with the protections, or it was a secret rule. Unlike in that airport with Albert though, I surrendered. I got out of the seat and did a walk of shame away from the ride. Beau got up, switched seats, and sat next to Hartford, who cried, "Why is Mommy going to jail?!"

I posted about this mini scandal on Instagram, and then the tabloid site Page Six ran a story titled "Stassi Schroeder: I was kicked off theme park ride for being pregnant." I'm sure there was more important news happening that day, but I guess Page Six thought they could get some clicks. My original Instagram Story about getting kicked off got a bunch of comments from strangers telling me what an irresponsible, horrible mom I was. I didn't see a sign saying pregnant ladies can't go on the slowest ride in history! What was going to happen? The ride would go so slow I would die of boredom? I wasn't trying to board Revenge of the Mummy, which goes like forty-five miles an hour. I just wanted to sit with my kid!

As frustrating as it can be, being treated like a delicate flower can have its perks, like when you're getting a seat on a subway or having every door held open for you. But all that care and worry from strangers goes away immediately after you give birth. Even the nurses in the hospital are like, "Okay, we did our job, good luck!" You're back in the real world where you can go on the *Secret Life of Pets* ride, but doors are slamming in your face and people are glaring at you because your kid is screaming. America treats mothers like shit. Beau's sister lives in Europe, and she tells me how much more respectful people are when it comes to pregnant women and parents, and I've seen enough TikToks that show how Europe embraces families and pregnant people. Like, those governments want to make life *easier* for parents. Can you imagine? Seriously, it's messed up. Even hotels over there are extra accommodating to families. Most of the hotels have rooms that are designed specifically for families. When we took Hartford to Paris, they even moved around the furniture to put in a super nice crib and decorate it like a nursery.

In Italy or Spain, for example, it's expected that you take your kids with you everywhere, even a 9:30 dinner (yes, dinner at 9:30 p.m.). Parents don't change their lives for their children; the children adapt to their parents' lives. I would get the weirdest looks if I were to take Hartford with us to a late dinner in the US. The thought of rolling up at the Polo Lounge at 9:00 p.m. with a toddler actually makes me laugh out loud. If I did that in America, someone would probably call child services on me. Also, I would never do that because a 9:00 p.m. dinner may as well be midnight at this point in life.

I know that in so many ways, I'm lucky. I work from home and have a nanny who comes to help. I have a hands-on partner who cooks and takes Hartford to school and who's there if I ever need a break. Let's say there are three categories of moms: stay-at-home moms, moms who work outside the home, and moms—like me—who work at home. Each one comes with its own unique set of guilt and issues. Being a full-time mom sounds way harder to me than anything. Going into work mode helps me feel like an actual adult with a brain that can do more than judge whether a diaper needs changing. Working away from home usually means asking a boss if you can leave to pick up your sick kid, or pumping in a broom closet during your lunch break. But working from home *with* kids, which is what I know, comes with its own forms of torture.

For example, if I'm behind a closed door recording our podcast and I hear Messer cry or Hartford yell, I feel guilty and get distracted and probably say something that makes zero sense because I'm thinking about my kids needing me instead of letting adult thoughts rule my brain. I'm sure they're fine because they're usually out there with our nanny or my mom, but in my mind I'm suddenly a terrible, neglectful parent who is more concerned with pop culture than baby poop (I mean, can you blame me?). Besides feeling guilty about my kids being on the other side of the door, as soon as they cry and I get distracted I feel like I've lost focus and I'm not doing the best work I can do. As a mom you kind of can't win. You can't tap out no matter what your situation is. Your brain is constantly making sure this little kid is alive, and that's exhausting! I chose this though. It's not like a supervillain swept into my life and forced me to have two beautiful children with a man I love and also have a career that fills me with happiness. It's not a brutal existence. I realize that. But still. I'm fucking tired!

Whenever a friend says they don't know if they want to have kids, I'm like, great! If you're iffy about it, quite literally *do not do it* because your entire life is going to change. Everything about you changes! Your hair, your body, your personality, your skin, your hormones, your feet, your brain chemistry . . . I could go on. You can say, "I'll still be me, I'm not going to change." Ha! Watching murder documentaries used to be my main hobby, but now that I have kids, murder docs give me way too much anxiety because I worry about my children getting murdered or becoming murderers. You can try your damnedest and I support your goals and your blind idealism (cute!), but you *will* change. It's not just your priorities that will shift. It trickles into everything else in your life—interests and hobbies change, your lifestyle changes, the places you go change. You are held hostage by your children for at least eighteen years, so you better want them and be okay with the fact that you *can* have a mimosa brunch with friends like once a year *but* there is a good chance you'll have to leave early because of a diaper blowout or an emotional meltdown or both at once.

So that's all to say that if you don't want kids, good for you!

This journey is not for everyone. Parenting is about survival. Forget the whole Crunchy Mom versus Silky Mom versus Scrunchy Mom. My category is Survival Mom.

I have to do what I can to survive, so if that means Hartford is going to have three cake pops in a row? Whatever. If it means that Beau and I have to sit quietly in a dark hotel room so our kids will nap and not have meltdowns when we take them into the world, fine! I love my kids and get a drug-induced high whenever I smell their heads. If you think that's weird, ask any parent if they do the same thing—they do! We all do. When they smile at me, my heart explodes like the Great Sept of Baelor in *Game of Thrones* (IYKYK). Still. There is an evolutionary reason babies and kids are cute. It's so we as parents can survive all the moments they make us miss our free, independent, fun, glorious child-free days before their cuteness changed our entire existence . . . *forever.*

I put my kids on Instagram, and I know some parents are extremely cautious about this, blurring out their children's faces or only showing the backs of their heads. That's great. Maybe those parents will win a Moral Compass Award or something, but my kids are cute. I want you to see their faces! The extreme version of this is the parents who put every moment online, creating TikToks about waking up seven times a night to calm a screaming baby. I'm fascinated by these "real-life" TikToks, even though a part of me is like, *I know this mom has a whole lighting setup in her baby's nursery so she can film.* It's fascinating, but also fucked-up. It does ease my mom guilt though to see another mom screwing up or struggling on camera for the whole world to see.

Maybe I started watching these videos a little too much though. One night when I was especially negative and tired, Beau said that watching these parents deal with all the hard stuff was affecting me in a negative way. Like it was just reminding me of everything hard instead of showing me happier, lighter moments. He said I should try *also* looking at parents who make it seem easy since I was getting caught up in how hard it could all be. This is what happens when you marry the son of a therapist, by the way. Anyway, I agreed that maybe I needed to look at serene cottagecore moms picking daffodils with kids in matching outfits instead of looking at a haggard mom in sweats holding an irate infant at 3:00 a.m. At least the daffodil-picking is inspirational, and maybe something to strive for. When I'm watching a mom with a screaming baby, instead of relaxing and getting some downtime, I'm just thinking, *I'm going to have to do that exact thing in about four hours.* It's just not helpful.

Even on my best days as a parent, guilt will hit me in some form. I asked Beau once if he feels guilt as a parent, like when he's so transfixed by a Rams game that he forgets he even has a family. His answer? "Not at all. I feel guilty that *you* feel mom guilt." Oh, how sweet. That must be so tough for him! Living a guilt-free life as a dad but then feeling bad for poor me. I know he means well, and it's not like I WANT him to be racked with guilt. He could have lied just a little and said, "I feel bad every time I cheer a touchdown." Points for honesty though.

Back in the day, people could say, "It takes a village to raise a child," and that would be true. Relatives all lived close by so you could hand the baby off to a grandparent or aunt or third cousin so you could work or run to the store, but now it's not like that at all. At least, not in Los Angeles, where most people moved from somewhere else far, far away, like Toledo. We still say that phrase, but no one actually lives it. In our culture we're just expected to do all these things on our own and not complain. When I complain about anything child-related on social media, I always get people who write, "Unfollowing! You should feel so lucky to have a kid." That is correct and I feel horrible complaining *but* that doesn't mean I have to pretend and put on a show that everything is easy. Are parents, and moms especially, not allowed to talk about the tough moments and the mental, emotional, and physical load of raising kids? Do we all have to put on a show for you? How twisted is that?

If you think the newborn and infant phases bring on the guilt, just wait until you enter the terrifying world of preschool. There is nothing like the glare (real or imagined) of a judgmental mother who is silently disapproving of the way you talk to/hold/feed/discipline/dress your child. You think the cliques in *Big Little Lies* were exaggerated? THINK AGAIN! Okay maybe they were a little exaggerated, but not by much. Also Los Angeles is a city that—besides New York—is probably at the top of the Scary Judgmental Moms population ranking, if *U.S. News & World Report* ever did a ranking like that, which it should. When Hartford was a toddler we were at a mommy-and-me class in Santa Monica. First of all, I can't believe I drove all the way to Santa Monica for a mommy-and-me class. Second of all, I remember some of the moms suddenly swarming me because I was the new one, their eyes wide, like they belonged to some cult where you exist on protein smoothies and Sancerre and nothing else.

"You have to take your daughter to Little Blossoms*," they each said. "It's the best preschool in the city. She *has* to go there . . ."

I started to think that if I didn't send Hartford to this Little Blossoms place, I would be failing her and ruining her life. Like a college or prospective spouse would one day say, "You didn't attend Little Blossoms? Be gone!" These moms were like a pack of benevolent, friendly Regina Georges, which is honestly on-brand for me, but I wasn't ready for all of this yet. I started to think that preschool was all about finding your mom friends, and had nothing to do with teachers or your kid or *learning and growing as a little human.* All of this new information scared the shit out of me! Honestly, to a certain extent, you do want to put your kid in a school where you like the parents, because when your kid starts going to school, you're going to be around those parents more than most of the friends you currently have. In my twenties, I probably would have been all about sending my child to Little Blossoms, but times had changed. Mostly, I just couldn't imagine driving my children all the way across town to play with a designer toddler kitchenette.

I told a friend who lived in New York about the experience, and she said that there was a preschool in Brooklyn where one of the moms said she'd lent a designer bag and a gold Rolex Daytona to another mom for the interview to get into the school. You need a designer bag and watch to get enrolled so your kid can eat

---

*   This is not a real school.

Tater Tots and play with a fake kitchen set all day? I mean I love a designer bag, but no, thank you. There was no way I would send my kids to a place like that. Beau and I found a sweet preschool that did not judge parents on their jewels and totes. Even then, the social anxiety I felt going to the first parent mixer was intense. I felt nervous all day. Like, do I ask these parents what they do for a living or is that rude? Do I dress casual, like a chill mom, or mildly dressed up, like a mom who means business? Once I got over my jitters, it actually ended up being fun, and the parents were thankfully cool and nice and no one mentioned Rolexes. I do feel guilty that I'm not doing Hartford's drop-off and pickup every day and Beau is doing most of them, but I'm home with the baby! I'm doing the best I can! See? The guilt is real.

A while back, I took Hartford to a dinner celebrating Lala's five years of sobriety. Brittany and Scheana were there with their kids, and after the cake came I looked over to see Scheana scraping the icing off the cake before her daughter, Summer Moon, ate it. This was happening while Hartford was busy shoving her second piece of cake—with icing—into her mouth. Again, it happened. Was I a bad mom, allowing my kid to have so much sugar? Should I be scraping icing off for my daughter so she could live a long, healthy life? But my kid loves icing. You can't undo that shit. The second that Hartford tried icing it was game over. Then I saw Scheana feeding her daughter *broccoli*. WTF! I tried the whole baby-led weaning thing, where you skip spoon-fed pureed food and go to safe finger foods, but now all my kid wants is mac 'n' cheese. All I can do is try to go easy on myself and remember that one day, hopefully soon, Hartford will eat some broccoli and that kids all over the world have eaten icing on cake since it was invented in 1655, and I should not feel like a failure for letting her shove two pieces into her cute little mouth. Let the girl have some joy.

Now, I *should* feel guilty for what I'm about to admit, but . . . I was INSANELY excited to discover I was having a boy. I've heard for so long that boys adore their moms, and Hartford legitimately bullies me sometimes. I'm totally aware that's maybe a selfish and/ or psycho reason to want a boy. I mean, the point of having kids isn't for them to provide us with love, it's for us to provide them with love. But still, I matter too, right?! And Hartford has always been a daddy's girl. Every time she would deny me a hug or kiss, I would remind her that she was about to have a baby brother and that she was missing the opportunity to get all the love and kisses just for her. If she didn't get the kisses in now, well then, I was just going to have to save them for him. Was that manipulative? Probably. But you gotta do what you gotta do to get your kid's affection sometimes, you know? It feels like it's a sort of weird karma or something that my daughter is so tough on me, that I must deserve it somehow, but it still hurts a little. What I'm really trying to say is, selfishly, I was excited to finally be someone's favorite in the house. What can I say? When it comes to my kids, I'm needy.

I will say that with a boy, I feel more pressure to raise him correctly, because statistically way more serial killers are men. The odds of Hartford becoming a murderer are a lot lower than Messer's odds. I guess I just feel like there's so much more room for error when you're raising a boy. Yes, I know girls can grow up to be

BRIBES
(70% EFFECTIVE)

legit monsters as well. But on top of trying to ensure that my son doesn't turn into a cannibal or something, I want to do my best to raise a man who treats women as respected equals. Is it too much to ask that men cherish us and handle us with care like we're delicate little flowers while also recognizing and respecting that we truly are the stronger gender and should be ruling the world?

MOMMY'S DWINK

There is so much pressure on parents—or at least on me, from me—to shape these humans, so my ultimate goal for my kids is that I want them to lead happy lives. I want them both to feel confident in being fully themselves. But yes I also want to raise a gentleman who knows how to treat women correctly. It would kill me if I found out I raised a fuckboy. Luckily Beau is *so* not an asshole, so I have faith that Messer will turn out okay. One of my worst fears is that I'll do my best and he'll still grow up and serial-kill people. If that happened, I would never forgive myself! I probably would bring him baked goods in prison though. But let's just say that by showing our kids love and trying to raise them with a solid moral compass while also

MOTHER, OH MOTHER!

PLEASE. JUST. SLEEP.

allowing them to eat icing, we are doing the best we can. In that, there should be zero guilt.

Things I Have Mom Guilt Over

✳ I feel guilty that one of my favorite parts of the day is when my kids are finally asleep. (But also, one of my other favorite parts is when they wake up in the morning.) How twisted is that?

✳ I 100 percent have mom guilt over the fact that Hartford eats mac 'n' cheese multiple times a week and that I'm not an organic food person.

✳ That we bribe her with ice cream and lollipops.

✳ That I bribe her with a present so I can clip her nails.

✳ That she's in school for most of the day and when she gets home, I'm mostly with the baby.

✳ I feel guilty that we don't have a yard and live on a hill, so if I'm not in the mood to go to the park, we watch a movie. I honestly feel guilty almost every time we watch TV or I hand her an iPad, aka the dreaded screen time debate.

✳ I feel guilty responding to texts/emails in front of my kids.

✳ I feel guilty that I'm not the one who cooks for the family. Like, how would we survive if we didn't have Beau? On that note, shout-out to single moms all day, every day.

✳ I feel guilty for wanting breaks.

✳ I feel guilty that when Hartford sees a wineglass any-where, she says, "Mommy's!!!"

✳ I feel guilty every time I raise my voice.

✳ I feel guilty that I've let her have the pacifier for so long, but it also breaks my heart to just take it from her when it brings her so much comfort.

✳ I feel guilt anytime I have ever left town without my children.

✳ I feel guilty we don't have a playroom, just a messy liv-ing room area.

✳ I feel guilt over putting Hartford in school right when her brother was born.

✳ I feel guilty when I talk about how hard being a parent can be.

✳ I feel guilty that I didn't breastfeed long enough.

✳ When I had Hartford, I would feel guilty when I did basic human things, like showering or taking time to get dressed.

✳ If I ever find that Hartford is in school and Messer is napping . . . I feel guilty when I allow myself to just sit and watch a show. There is this voice in my head that says I should always be doing something. Maybe that's a habit left over from SUR, because when you work in restaurants, if you're slow, you feel like you should be polishing a ketchup bottle or dusting a ceiling fan during your downtime.

✳ I feel major guilt that I'm enabling Hartford by the way I handle her tantrums.

✳ I feel guilty when we have a day at home together and I'm not fully present because I'm just . . . tired.

✳ I feel guilty when I put my kids down to bed and they're still awake. Like, when I look in the baby monitors and I see they're still awake, it makes me feel like the worst mom ever. Like I feel guilty that they're alone in their room, when they are totally fine. IT MAKES NO SENSE.

✳ I feel guilty I get so annoyed with Messer when he doesn't stop fussing. He's a poor little baby who can't communicate, and I still get frustrated.

✳ I feel guilty there are 987,349 times more photos of Hartford as a baby than there are of Messer.

✳ I feel guilty that I don't like the newborn phase.

✳ I feel guilty I don't do Hartford's baths anymore, because I'm doing Messer's.

✳ I feel guilty when I'm working, because I'm not with one of my kids. But when I'm just with my kids, I feel guilty I'm not working.

✳ I feel guilty I don't have my children FaceTime their family members enough.

✳ I feel guilty when I get bored from playing games or reading a book with them.

✳ I feel guilty every time I hear Hartford say "Mommy work" when Beau tells her why I'm leaving to go somewhere.

✳ I feel guilty that when I leave the house to go somewhere other than work, somewhere that's fun for me, I still have to tell her I'm going to work.

✳ I feel guilty that I get bored at the park sometimes.

✳ I feel guilty when we don't leave the house because I think it's too hot outside.

✳ I feel guilty for feeling guilty, and I also feel guilty writing this list instead of playing with my kids.

Takeaway

Mom guilt is a beast. If you never feel it, please share your secret with the world because you must be the ONLY ONE. Or you're a sociopath. I'm trying to remember that you can't be everything, all the time, for your kids. There is no perfect school, no perfect way to parent, and letting them eat icing on cake does not mean you're a monster. It means you're a parent who knows that icing is delicious. They'll eat broccoli . . . one day.

· CHAPTER 7 ·

Back to Reality (Sort Of)

For as long as I can remember, I have been a JOMO girlie (joy of missing out). I know it might not have seemed that way if you watched *Vanderpump Rules* and assumed I was out every night (and day), but as I've said 8,657 times: I'll take a couch, a blanket, and a romantic historical drama over a club or party any day. When I was fired by Bravo though, I started to feel FOMO creeping into my life, at least in terms of work. I wasn't allowed to do the things I used to do, like show up to film a scene with my friends, or get a paycheck. That life was no longer an option for me, so this experience of feeling like I was missing out was new. I'd tied so much of my identity to my job, to being on reality TV, and suddenly that was gone. At that time when it all first happened, I had no idea that I would kind of, sort of, in a roundabout way, get asked if I wanted to come back to the show.

Growing up, I always looked up to my mom for being a work-ingwoman. I thought it was cool. Her 1990s Romy and Michele business suits, her big hair, the fact that she managed restaurants like a boss. She did a little bit of everything when I was growing up, and I always felt proud that I had a mom who was running shit. At least it seemed that way to me. My friends' moms who didn't work were more involved in the school or sports or dance, but I never felt resentful. I remember being at Mardi Gras one year with my friends when I was about eleven years old. Before you start clutching your pearls thinking me and my fifth-grade friends were flashing strangers for purple bead necklaces, if you grow up in New Orleans you basically start going to Mardi Gras the second you leave the birth canal. It's family friendly too, at least, before dark. Anyway, my friends and I were talking about what we wanted our style to be like when we grew up. I said I wanted to dress like a businesswoman, like my mom. That would be my look: a confident boss bitch, minus the pastels.

In 2015, a Harvard Business School professor surveyed fifty thousand adults in twenty-five countries, and found that having a working mother actually benefits children when they get older— especially daughters. The study showed that girls with employed moms went on to do better in their careers. So, thank you, Mom! The study results don't mean that every single woman who had a working mom will never have setbacks (like, say, getting fired from a reality TV show), *but* it proves that the mom guilt is a waste of time, and that showing your kids what a boss bitch looks like can be good for them. I try to remember this every time I feel bad that

I'm recording a podcast or writing and my kids start to cry. One day, they'll think of me as a badass . . . I hope. Also, stay-at-home moms truly do have the hardest job in the world, and I wish more people viewed what they do as work, and not just work but *the toughest work.*

When my mom married my dad, she did enter that stay-at-home mom life for a while. My dad's family belonged to a country club in Los Angeles, so my mom would buy Chanel shoes at Neiman's so she'd fit in with the tennis crowd. She says their relationship fell apart because he found out about all the handbags and shoes she'd been buying to fit in, and he made her return them. So, like a million other married couples, a major problem was money issues. When they divorced, my mom went back to work as a makeup artist for Prescriptives, which was kind of like the Glossier of its day. She was part of a team that would travel to weekend conventions with a well-known makeup artist. Once she was free from the pressures of country club life, my mom never splurged on bags or shoes. She did splurge on traveling. She took us to Europe, which, looking back, probably shaped my personality in a lot of ways.

When I was twelve years old my mom took me to Venice and Paris, and I remember taking the overnight train between cities. We stayed up late playing cards (in our hotel, not at a casino), talking, and doing each other's hair. I have photos of her in the train cabin with her hair in pigtails, drinking from a bottle of champagne. Talk about goals! In Venice she took me to the iconic Caffè Florian for hot chocolate. The place is more than three hundred years old, so maybe that's why I love old buildings and architecture so much. My mom also got me a pair of black leather knee-high boots, and when I wore those back in New Orleans I felt like the most fashionable preteen who'd ever existed. We went to the Louvre in Paris, and I saw the Egyptian antiques collection because I was obsessed with the movie *The Mummy*. My mom took photos of me in front of the Eiffel Tower because I wanted to look like the Olsen twins in *Passport to Paris*. In my preteen mind, if these were the experiences a workingwoman could buy for herself and her child, I would be a workingwoman. At the end of the trip my mom took me on a treasure hunt around Paris for a specific bottle of wine that she just *had* to bring back to New Orleans. This woman made room in her suitcase for WINE. Actually my mom told me it was a special handpainted vintage bottle of Veuve Clicquot. Like I said, my mom worked hard, and this is what it got her. She was girlbossing so she could bring vintage champagne home to Louisiana, *and* make her kid feel like an Olsen twin.

My mom worked hard after that divorce, and I always felt protective of her. I worried that other moms who didn't have jobs might've been looking down on her. It was a privilege to not work and to have long gossipy lunches with friends every day.

As proud as I was of my mom, in my brain it was like the more a mom worked the poorer the family was. If someone's mom was a stay-at-home mom, to me, that meant they were very wealthy. I've joked that my parents have married so many times, it's like they did it for sport, like it was a competition. Not to see who could stay married, but who could marry the most times. The stepmom I had during my most formative years (preteens, teens, and early adulthood) was a workaholic. She was in public relations and had major boss bitch vibes. She was the kind of person who worked out during lunch breaks and dieted constantly, even though she was blessed with supermodel genetics. She was always on her Palm Pilot, which drove my grandparents crazy. Did she care that her in-laws were annoyed that she was a busy PR woman glued to technology? Hell no. We didn't always get along great, maybe because being a stepmom is a ridiculously complicated role to have, or maybe it wasn't her top priority in life. It was just below being successful, thin, busy, and well-dressed. One day, after about seven years of marriage, she just went home and told my dad she was leaving, and I never saw her again. She did send me one of her watches, maybe because that was more convenient to her than actually communicating with me. So after she decided to vanish from our lives, I wouldn't necessarily call her a role model of mine. And also, if you have to skip lunch for a workout and shut human contact out of your life so you can poke a Palm Pilot to be successful, I would rather just chill. Still, she was one of my early examples of what it meant to be a grown woman, so some of her workaholic vibes had to have rubbed off on me.

My mom worked because she loved it, but she also worked because she had to. My grandmother, on the other hand, loved to work, period. End of story. She was *technically* a stay-at-home mother to six children for most of her life, but she always went to work for my grandfather's business as much as she could. She was one of those women who loved to be busy and to scratch things off her to-do list. During World War II, she worked as an accountant for a lawyer, and then when my grandfather came back from the war and started his business working as a real estate developer, she did his bookkeeping and kept track of every penny. She was meticulous and on top of everything, all the time. She was hands down the most responsible human being I've ever known. A true Capricorn: hardworking, organized, good with money. And then there's me. I was the WORST with money, and it drove my grandmother crazy. She would never throw anything away, even plastic shopping bags. She had cabinets full of them. She loved a deal and a sale. To me, things like Black Friday sales are my worst nightmare. I just buy crap I don't need because it says SALE. I used to spend a whole night of tips from SUR on pizza and wine, even though I had credit card debt. I'm better now, but it took me a while to get the whole "financial responsibility" thing.

I remember my first day of college at LSU, I was walking with my friend Sheena Mannina, and there was a Chase Bank right by our apartment complex. They were giving away free sweatshirts to college kids who signed up for a credit card, and I wanted a sweatshirt, so I signed up. It was free money! I learned that I could *also* get an Express credit card, so pretty soon I had a huge amount of debt. It was probably around $25,000, and I didn't pay it all off until season three of *Vanderpump Rules*, because I finally made enough. It only took me seven years to get to that point.

I wrote about early jobs I had as a barista or a server in my previous books. I've also written all about being on *Vanderpump*. Ah, Bravo. The place that gave me a career and a paycheck for eight glorious seasons. Well, mostly glorious. I had my moments. Like the time I had a drunken meltdown in the French Quarter of New Orleans during Katie and Tom's bachelor/bachelorette trip. Or the night I started sobbing after consulting with an actual witch about my Dark Passenger behavior. Being on reality TV is not as common of a career as becoming a lawyer or going into marketing, but it's what I knew. And for so many years, I freaking loved it. What I didn't realize until I was off the show and in the actual real world is that when you're on a show like that, your emotional intelligence goes way down. Like, down to the bottom of the ocean where no animals or plants can survive except goblin sharks and sea cucumbers. Because you get all this attention from producers and then the public for every little thing you do or say, you get used to thinking that everything you do or say matters and everyone on the planet cares. You become so self-absorbed that when you're having conversations with other people all you do is focus on yourself. Think about it. You know those straight-to-camera confessionals you see on reality shows? The ones where we talk about *every single little thing* that's happening in the episode? How could that not make you feel like EVERYTHING in your life is IMPORTANT?

Once the spotlight shuts off and you're living like a regular human and not doing confessionals to camera, you realize that not everything you feel or think matters to other people. Suddenly, it's a much better conversation if you ask another person how *they* feel or what *they* think. This might not sound revolutionary to the 98 percent of the population that's not on reality TV, but I'm telling you, that's what happens when you're on a show like that, especially when you start in your early twenties. You don't realize it's unhealthy because you're getting all this attention and money for doing it. Now that I've been away from that world, I guess I realize that it can turn your idea of success into a twisted version of just being a raving narcissist. So to anyone I ever spoke to but only focused on myself: I am so fucking sorry!

I'm not saying I hated and regret being on the show. That's not the case at all. I loved doing it, and I'm grateful for the years I had on *Vanderpump*. I met some of my best friends and had some of the best (and worst) times of my life. I made a living. It's not that I would never do reality TV again, but that I wouldn't do *that* type of reality TV, the kind that thrives on drama and shadiness and toxic fights that erupt after you've been drinking for six hours straight. I would do it if it accurately and honestly reflected what my life is like now. I don't want to change for a show, and I definitely don't want to start going to clubs and causing drama. Now that I have kids and my life is more about diaper changes than changing outfits fifteen times before I head out to a party, I sometimes wonder what our lives would be like if Beau and I *were* still on *Vanderpump*. We probably would have been put in situations that would have caused fights that we wouldn't have had in real life. The producers probably would have scheduled a million "boys' night out" scenes while I was pregnant so that I would rage on Beau, so people would worry that our relationship was imploding. A big, sober, hormonal, pregnant Stassi going ballistic would have been their ultimate goal. It might be good for ratings, but it's not a healthy way to live.

Like I said though, I would do it again *if* it were a different type of show. And I *almost* did it again when I was kind of, sort of asked about being back on *Vanderpump*.

Right around the time that my second book, *Off with My Head*, was announced, I got a call out of the blue from one of my old *Vanderpump* producers. He started with some small talk, asking how Beau and I were doing, and then he got to the point. He was calling to get my thoughts on coming back to the show. The same show that had fired me in 2020. The same show that had given me a career and a feeling of success and accomplishment, and that then went and gave me a feeling of being the exact opposite of a girlboss. He listed out all the reasons he thought I should come back to the show, and was so persistent we started arguing over the phone. Sure, having my salary back would be nice, but it wasn't a simple decision, considering everything that happened. He was pushing, almost sounding desperate, like if I came back to the show and there were big, dramatic headlines about my return, the show would continue. It was intense.

When he asked the question, my heart fluttered and sank at the same time. I had a book that was about to come out, and Beau and I had our *The Good the Bad the Baby* podcast, but that was it. I felt so done with *Vanderpump*, so then why was I having this visceral reaction? It was a feeling of total dread mixed with a feeling of *Do I actually need this?* Would this be my opportunity to work? Will it be the only chance I ever get? Was he actually asking me back to the show or . . .

"I just want you to know this isn't a formal offer," he added.

Oh. Okay.

"Can we at least go to dinner and talk about it?"

I agreed to the dinner, even though it was a mindfuck of a phone conversation. I spent the days and nights between the call and the dinner trying to figure out how I really felt about the whole thing. Was I closer to the "no way in hell" side of the spectrum or the "I'll report to set at 7:00 a.m. to collect a paycheck and a sense of self-worth" side? I truly did not know. In so many ways, saying yes would feel like taking a million steps backward. Since getting fired, I'd done so much work on myself, which sounds cringey, I know. But I had. I'd worked through the pain of getting fired, looked at my own behaviors—which I wasn't proud of—and started finding ways to grow and be happy that had nothing to do with the show. I was actually enjoying my life.

I wasn't and am not the same person, so I'm probably not even cut out for *Vanderpump* anymore. My confessionals now would be about getting up at 4:00 a.m. to feed a crying baby, or feeling mom guilt about recording a podcast. I don't want to get drunk and fight with people anymore, which was one of my main claims to fame. Did I want to go back to a show that was now kind of a sinking ship (this was before Scandoval, which I'll get to soon enough)?

Also, I'd spent the entire day that my book was announced sitting in Hartford's ball pit feeling like I was going to vomit, worrying that a barrage of comments like "This is trash!" or "Stassi is evil!" would come through. Instead, the comments were supportive. I was beginning to realize that maybe *Vanderpump* wouldn't be my last chance at a career.

I went through all the pros and cons, and then the day of the dinner came. By then, I was fully prepared to look at the producer and say, "No, I won't come back to the show. I have more to offer than drunk fighting!" For the dinner, I wore my standard "feel good about myself but also mean business" uniform: an oversize blazer with a sweater mini dress underneath, plus brown crocodile knee-high leather boots. When in doubt, an oversize blazer is a safe space, I swear. I felt like I was still that cool, young, stylish Stassi, just maybe more mature, more elevated, with my shit a little more together than before. Then the producer shows up, sits down, puts his napkin in his lap, and says, "Hi. Well, I spoke too soon . . ."

What. The. Fuck!

I didn't get to have my big triumphant moment at all. He told me that someone from *Real Housewives of Salt Lake City* had just been fired, so it wasn't the right time to go back to Bravo about bringing me back. I had understood he wasn't giving me a formal offer on the phone, but he hadn't even spoken to Bravo? He was just testing me before he went to them, and then this happened and he backed down. I played it off like I didn't care, but inside of my protective blazer I was fuming. I was season-one Stassi four pinot grigios in and pissed, but this time, you would never know. I wasn't secretly fuming because I wanted to go back. I was fuming because what if I'd gotten my hopes up? What if I had gotten excited and pinned some financial and personal and professional decisions on this? I'm not saying I am a victim here. I know I got myself canceled, and I deeply regret the decisions I made. But this whole thing was so disturbing, like what if I had fallen back into that mode of thinking *Vanderpump* was something I needed to feel happy or successful, and then it was pulled away? I was so thankful I had already come to the decision I had, otherwise my confidence would have been destroyed, the same as it had been in 2020. So we had dinner, I kept my cool, and I went home to my family. Beau made me a Disaronno on the rocks, and I crawled into Hartford's ball pit (another safe space). From the ball pit, I told Beau all about the dinner, and I chose to celebrate the fact that the book announcement for *Off with My Head* had gone so well instead of spiraling over the dinner. I posted photos of myself in the ball pit on Instagram, and if you saw those photos, you would just think I was hard-core celebrating the book news, and have no clue about the dinner.

So, all that said—remember when I mentioned that *Vanderpump* had gotten boring and lame? Well, then Scandoval came along. I'll never forget what I was doing when I heard the news. I was going through my clothes I planned to sell, since I was pregnant and in the process of giving up my closet to my baby. I was taking photos of the different dresses and skirts when I saw the news on Instagram. At first I didn't believe it. It sounded insane to me. Tom and Ariana had been what I thought was a solid couple—they had always stood up for each other. I'd heard other people say they were more like roommates, but Ariana and I were never close and Tom Sandoval and I have always hated each other, so what did I know? I immediately texted my friends on the show to see if the rumors were true, and they all said yes. Ariana and I were not in touch, but I felt like I was thrown right back into the show since suddenly people were asking what I thought or if I knew. I had tried with Ariana over the years, and I felt like at one time we had a lot in common. Tom Sandoval and I never got along, so I wondered if she didn't like me because he told her not to. I always felt like he was holding her back, so when I read about Scandoval I thought the world was her oyster now, she could do whatever she wanted to do. I hadn't watched the show in a long time, but I watched the new episodes. I admit it was kind of hard to watch it and to see the show getting popular again, being on the outside. It's messed up, I know. I'm allowed to care and to also feel that work FOMO. Let me live! Watching it again though, I also felt like, they're *still* being shady and fighting and bringing all this drama? We did things like cheat on people and cry on camera in our twenties, but . . . that was then?

After the news broke, Taylor called me that Friday and was like, "You know we have to talk about Scandoval on the podcast next week, right?" Taylor and I did these bits on the *Straight Up with Stassi* podcast called "Pop Culture Hour" where we would gossip about whatever new gossip had invaded everyone's feeds that week. I had not talked about *Vanderpump* in so long, and I did not want to start, but . . . it was SCANDOVAL. People's grandparents knew about it. Aliens knew about it, probably. It blew up to the point that we could not ignore it. It actually would have been weird not to talk about it. I was so nervous I started that episode by blurting out, "I'm pregnant again!"

I wrote about what I would say for two whole days before we recorded. I hadn't spoken about the show publicly, so it felt odd. Also, the whole thing was a little triggering. Like I said to Taylor, the scandal was bigger than Armie Hammer being a would-be freaking cannibal. Plus, Tom was just diabolical. Maybe more diabolical than a cannibal. I didn't know Raquel well, but I do remember her being extremely nervous every time we interacted on the show. Her voice shook. She seemed so sweet, and I could not imagine someone who was so nervous and almost timid doing what she did to Ariana. Whenever I filmed with Raquel, I would think to myself, *What are you doing here? You are way too sweet and are not cut out for this.* And then Scandoval happened. Taylor and I were #TeamAriana all the way. I mean, the guy dressed up as Raquel one Halloween when he was still with Ariana. How deranged is that?! I don't even think someone like Ted Bundy or Charles Manson would have done that. Yes, they murdered, but would they have dressed as their mistress on Halloween in front of their girlfriend? That's just dark.

We may be talking about Scandoval for the rest of our lives. It might turn into folklore, a story passed down from generation to generation. But there is plenty to talk about in pop culture besides *Vanderpump*. It's okay to have nuanced feelings about what having it all means when it comes to career. I can feel that FOMO but also feel totally relieved that my life is different. You can get all nostalgic about your twenties but also feel thankful as hell you don't ever have to go back to that era. The more distance I get from *Vanderpump*, the more fulfilled I am now in *this* moment. One thing I will say about Scandoval is that I had a whole new generation of people who'd never seen early *Vanderpump Rules* seasons finding it and following me, which I guess was technically good for business. Who would think that two people on a TV show breaking up because of a horrible, gross affair would positively impact the business of someone who was not even involved? I'll just accept that as my going-away gift.

Maybe being on a reality show is not the job or the life that most people on the planet have, but most people on the planet can relate to *moving on*. There may be opportunities or situations that seem ideal, but if a boss or CEO or manager or producer doesn't truly want you on their team, find something else. I know that might be easier said than done, but sometimes having it all means realizing your worth, and understanding that having something else might be way better than what you had before.

CHAPTER 8

What Is Success FOMO and How to Get Rid of It

et's be real—we've all been guilty of this. You see another woman who is similar to you. She may be around the same age, or maybe you grew up together, or maybe you're just in the same career field. You're scrolling through Instagram, and you see her post about some major career success. You're happy for her, sure, but you suddenly start to spiral and feel insecure. You begin questioning yourself and why you haven't accomplished certain things. You keep reminding yourself that this woman *deserves* this. You're happy for her, dammit! So why are you spiraling?

I call that Success FOMO.

I totally used to suffer from Success FOMO. The irony is that I felt it the most in 2019, during my girlboss year. I was on TV, had a podcast, a wine brand, a fiancé, a *New York Times* bestselling book, and an animated series in the works that was about basic witches who could turn a bottle of ranch into a wand with magical powers.

You would think that because I was doing so much I would feel like it was enough. But that's the thing about the girlboss mentality. It's never enough. There's always more success to be had, more to accomplish.

I often wondered why I suffered from Success FOMO. It's not to say I wasn't happy for my peers when good opportunities came to them. I was. But at the same time, I would be overcome by insecurity if the same things weren't happening for me. My earliest memories of Success FOMO begin with *Vanderpump Rules*. I don't ever remember feeling this way in high school or college. I started the show with my actual friends as servers, all of us on the same level. It's like *Vanderpump* was a thousand-yard dash, and before it aired, we were all standing in our spots at the starting line waiting to race one another. We didn't set out to race, but whether we liked it or not, that's what ended up happening. I think it was because there is such a focus from the media on who is going to be the breakout star of a series. It all starts from there, and then once you *are* a breakout star, the network and your producers and everyone around you puts the pressure on you to not lose those qualities that made audiences pay attention to you. There's always that pressure to maintain, and to outperform previous seasons. And on top of that, it's hard not to compare yourself to your peers when you're all friends who started at the very same spot.

I remember the exact moment I was cured of Success FOMO. It was after I became a mom, after I was fired from my jobs, during that time when I was soul-searching. I was listening to *The Skinny Confidential Him & Her* podcast with Lauryn and Michael Bosstick. They were on the topic of jealousy, and one of them said something along the lines of: If you are jealous of something that someone else has, then imagine you would have to switch lives completely with that person in order to have that one thing. I'm talking about switching partners, switching children, switching bodies, switching EVERYTHING. There's no point in being jealous of something that happens for someone unless you're perfectly happy to switch your entire life with theirs.

That seriously hit home. I had just had Hartford, and the thought of not having her, my husband, my life, my family, who I was, all of it . . . that pretty much cured me of Success FOMO. After that, when I saw something good happen for one of my peers, even though I was sitting at home just praying I could work again someday, all I had to do was think of switching lives with that person and everything that came along with it, and I felt zero jealousy. This all comes down (again) to gratitude and being so grateful for everything that makes up your life.

Just because I've found my own ways to combat and cure most cases of Success FOMO, it doesn't mean I'm entirely immune. I'm a human being after all, and there have still been times I've had to just give in to the Success FOMO and soak in it. For example, January 7, 2024, which happened to be my daughter's third birthday. You're probably wondering why I was suffering from Success FOMO on a special day like that. Well, the Creative Arts Emmy Awards happened to fall on the same exact day. And *Vanderpump Rules* had been nominated for an Emmy for the very first time. It was obviously a total bummer that some of my friends couldn't make Hartford's birthday party because they were going to be glammed up in gorgeous gowns attending a cool award show, but that wasn't why it truly stung. I don't get jealous about things like BravoCon because I've been there, done that. I have FOMO when the show reaches new heights. I would have LOVED to have gone to the Emmys.

Minor Things That Set Me Off

* When I find multiple baseball caps lying everywhere in the house. I read that there are two types of people: people who don't like messes and people who don't like dirt. Beau can't stand dirt, and will vacuum nonstop, but I can't stand messes. I need things to visually look like they're tidy and in the right place. When I find four to five baseball caps sprinkled all over the house, it annoys the shit out of me.

HATS. EVERYWHERE.

RAMS

* Bad hair day with my cowlick for sure. Cowlicks are the worst, let's just call them for what they are . . . they're

the devil's work. The devil's stamp. That's the only explanation that makes sense to me, because there's no way God or whomever allows cowlicks to exist; they make styling my own hair impossible 90 percent of the time.

HASHTAG EMBARRASSED (ARE HASHTAGS STILL A THING?)

✳ When my gels start peeling, I become insufferable and my day is ruined.

✳ When the formula machine is out of water. It's a rule in my house to add more water to the formula machine if you're the last one to use it when it gets empty. The wrath I feel when I've woken up with Messer in the middle of the night to find the formula machine out of water . . .

✳ When my dog pees outside the pee pad and I step in it. It makes no sense. Like why?

✳ When I'm really excited about a show and I think it's bingeable on Netflix, but then I find out it's Apple TV+ and I have to wait every week for a new episode.

✳ When I Postmates Starbucks and I order things for my family also, but they forget my coffee, which was the whole reason I ordered it in the first place.

✳ When I pay for the Gogo in-flight Wi-Fi on the plane, but it still doesn't work properly. That shit is so expensive, you would think the internet would be lightning fast, but nope.

✳ When I'm stalking someone's social media and I accidentally "like" something from way back. I mean, I have only myself to blame, but it seriously is a day ruiner.

✳ People who photoshop or airbrush only themselves in a group photo. Y'all need to be shot out of Earth's atmosphere; we don't have space for you here.

✳ When my contact gets stuck in the corner of my eye because I was too aggressive with my makeup wipe. I legit go into a panic that it'll be stuck there forever. Every. Single. Time.

I spiraled because I had spent eight years on that show, given it my all, and would've died to have the show be nominated while I was on it. That was always a goal of ours. When I spiral, I obsess. The thing I'm spiraling about is the only thing I can talk about or think about. I tried all the normal tricks I had to combat the feeling, but ultimately I just had to give in to that sulky, jealous feeling for a finite amount of time. I allowed myself to bitch and complain the day before her birthday, but once I woke up on her birthday, it was all about Hartford. The odds of this award show being scheduled for the exact timing of my daughter's third birthday were honestly poetic. Like, of course it was.

So if you're finding you can't talk yourself out of Success FOMO, give yourself a break. A little jealousy every now and then is normal, right?! Just be sure to move past it, and don't let it consume you.

Now, in case that little trick doesn't work for you and you still find yourself green with envy over your coworker's promotion, here are some tips:

❋ It takes more energy to be jealous than to be happy, so why waste that precious energy? What are you actually accomplishing by being jealous? When you let those negative vibes creep in, they inform everything you do, and they cast a black cloud over your day and take away energy you could be putting toward your partner or kids or friends. And who wants to go through the day with a black cloud? Unless it's Halloween, and you're wanting to lean into spooky season, then, of course, duh. Basically, you're only hurting yourself when you're jealous, so let that shit go.

❋ Ask yourself this: Is the thing you're having Success FOMO over *actually* exactly what you want? Maybe ideally it sounds like something you would want for yourself, but really . . . is it? Maybe this thing you think you want comes with longer work hours, or a significant amount of added pressure. Maybe the commute is hell. Make sure all the details surrounding this thing are details that would make *you* happy, not someone else. If you're obsessing over an ex's new relationship, try to remember that the new person has to be with your ex. Yikes.

✳ If all else fails, try BDE. If you've tried everything else, if you've focused on the things you're grateful for, if nothing is working, then just try a little bit of delusional energy and have a personal day doing all of your favorite things. When I take a personal day and decide to put aside my responsibilities for the day and go to brunch, go shopping, maybe get a lymphatic drainage massage, those things always make me feel freaking great about myself. Just spend your day channeling your inner Sofia Richie— someone who became an It Girl not for working hard but for just socializing and being fabulous—and do whatever the heck you want.

✳ You can also use BDE as a tool to simply decide that the other person's life just isn't all that great, or not great enough to be jealous of. Maybe they're the one who is exhausted and having FOMO about *you*. Is that delusional? Possibly. But it might actually help.

Takeaway

We've all felt it (unless you are the most selfless and angelic being on the planet): that moment you feel insanely jealous of someone else. But one day, you'll be the person inspiring the FOMO, so chill. We can "have it all" in moments, but not all the time. And remember that when you find yourself coveting what someone else has or what they've accomplished, ask yourself if you would completely switch lives with them. Chances are, the honest answer will be *no*. Even if it's Meghan Markle. Maybe.

CHAPTER 9

Mom Friends Forever! (Or Not)

I have a confession to make, so brace yourselves. I like kid birthday parties more than I like most adult birthday parties. I like some adult parties, but now I can't just sling a purse over my shoulder and head out the door, I have to find a babysitter or make sure the nanny can be there. It's an ordeal and a commitment. Maybe I'm okay with kid parties because most of the kid birthday parties I've gone to so far have been at leafy outdoor parks or in backyards, and not at crowded indoor trampoline parks with ball pits full of eight thousand germs, or—evil of all evils—at a Chuck E. Cheese. I haven't been subjected to greasy pizza and two hours of pretending you're wildly entertained watching your child play Whac-a-Mole as a way to avoid awkward small talk with a parent you barely know. So, yeah, I like kid birthdays. Before you write me off as a masochist, let me explain why I *also* sometimes dread them. Two emotions can coexist, okay! It's complicated.

Since Hartford started getting invited to birthdays, my social anxiety has found a new reason to kick into overdrive. Based on the amount of stress I experience before baby and toddler parties, you'd think I was raised in a dark cave with zero human contact. Kid birthday parties are a breeding ground for social awkwardness. I mean, for the most part, I don't know most of the parents. I spent the first year of my daughter's life pretty much sheltering in place at home. So when we go to a party it feels like I'm walking into some singles mixer, except instead of trying to make some romantic connection, I'm trying to make a mom friend connection. Or, honestly, just trying to be the best mom version of myself so that the other moms don't go talking mom-shit behind my back. Just like a singles mixer, everything about these parties feels forced. I quite literally never know what to say to a new mom at a birthday party. Do I ask what she does for a living? Do I ask her parenting style? Do I ask how long her labor was? Her favorite food? Favorite movie? Is she a free-range parent or a snowplow?! I need someone to point me in the right direction, and maybe give me a list of mom-friendly conversation starters.

Let's start simple.

Is that your kid?

If the answer is no, then move along.

If yes, then continue with follow-up questions:

Is that your only kid? Oh you have two? What's the age difference? How was that having two under two?

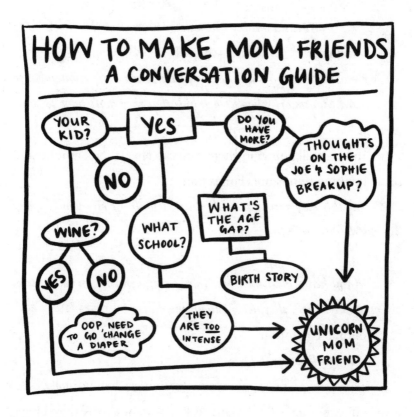

Do y'all live in the area? Where are you kids in school? Getting your kids in the right schools, I mean, it's a jungle out there. Amirite?!

Side note: I've never met a mom who didn't like sharing or hearing about birth stories and postpartum recovery. Myself included. It's like we've all been a part of some ritual blood bond circle or something. So when all else fails, ask about her postpartum recovery or whether she liked her ob-gyn.

Once we've established some sort of situation, I then tend to ask for advice. It helps to be self-deprecating. I feel like moms just want to know other moms are hanging on by a thread too:

My kid won't eat anything but mac 'n' cheese, what did you do to get your kid to snack on roasted seaweed?

We're going through a no-sharing phase, and I don't know what to do. I heard Montessori schools teach kids that they don't have to share ever?

If these are all going nowhere, you can always look around and see if anything stands out. For example:

Wow, this playground is really shitty, I wish the city would spend our tax dollars on fixing it up.

Or:

Did you hear about the house that got broken into on Lark Street the other day? Yeah, they never caught the dude.

Honorable mention:

So, do you like wine?

My favorite part of a mom conversation is when it finally takes a turn into pop culture. I want to know what shows they binge, which celebrity breakup they're sad about, who their favorite Tik-Toker is. I'll find a way to test the waters by saying something like "Oh my goodness, your daughter's hair looks just like Ariana Grande's, so beautiful!" If the mom responds with something like "Oh, thank you. By the way, I can't believe that guy she's having the affair with was married with a baby." Then I know she's my kind of mom friend.

When I do finally find someone I can have a conversation with, I start to worry that I'm taking up too much of her time, like I'm taking her away from her *actual* mom friends. You want the interaction to be long enough so that it's somewhat meaningful but short enough so that you're not that person the other moms are trying to avoid. "Watch out, Stassi is coming over here; it'll be a forty-minute conversation about *Gilmore Girls*. . . ."

I mean, my ideal mom friend would want to talk about *Gilmore Girls* for forty minutes, but I have yet to meet her.

I feel like every single mom at the party has a game plan, myself included. There is intention and strategy behind every decision. Honestly, women should've been the ones drawing up war and battle plans over the course of history. We're constantly calculating, observing, planning, even at a toddler's "Two Infinity and Beyond" birthday party. But let's just take the whole "I have anxiety because I don't know the other parents" element out of it for a second. Even when I'm going to a kid's birthday party where I am already friends with the other parents, I get anxious about the fact that there is a pretty sizable chance that my child might decide on that very day to act like a feral animal who had just been let out of her cage. And then whatever meltdown or hysteria happens feels like a reflection on me and how I am as a parent. This situation has resulted in me running after Hartford to corral her while simultaneously embarking on some sort of apology tour to all the other parents.

After all of that, how can kid birthday parties possibly still trump adult parties? It's because at children's birthday parties, I have armor. I have a shield. I have an indisputable defense as to why I need to end a conversation or leave early. That shield is my children. There's nothing better than using your kid as an excuse to avoid an awkward conversation with someone. Like "Oh, I'm so sorry! I need to go check on Hartford, it looks like she needs a sip of water." Or "I apologize, I need to go change Messer's diaper for forty-five minutes." At adult parties, I have no excuses for anything. I just have to sit in whatever social awkwardness I've found myself in—or created. Having kids is like having wingmen at parties. You always have someone there with you for backup, and you always have a semi-legit reason to make a French exit/Irish goodbye.

For months after Hartford was born, I wanted a millennial mom friend who was about my age, who would accept my quirks, and who would not judge me for handing my child a cake pop to calm her down. I very luckily found this unicorn mom friend *right next door.* We were both pregnant during Covid lockdowns, and Beau and I would see her husband outside sometimes. He and Beau would talk all the time, so naturally I decided to do some online stalking and find out who his wife was. I found this intimidatingly beautiful woman on Instagram, and her bio just said: *I'm a lurker.*

I'm a lurker?! WTF! Who the hell was living next door? A gorgeous peeping Tom? A hot murderess? I had to find out more. I discovered that she had recently made a short film called *Millennial Mom,* so the fact that we were part of the same generation was a good omen. When Hartford was born I would take her out in her stroller and I would see my neighbor, who was still pregnant, out walking. After she had her daughter, I decided to invite them for a playdate. If you peeked inside my windows and saw me getting ready for this playdate, you might have mistaken me for a hardened military general drawing up a plan of attack. I was making an actual effort to make a new friend, which is not easy when you get older. It's not like you meet friends just because you're both twenty-two and drunk in a club bathroom. Making friends when you're a parent and over the age of, say, thirty, is serious business.

I was so nervous before my neighbor came over. Would she want snacks? Like, a bag of pretzels or an actual charcuterie board? Cocktails? Wine? Do I need to have a mom-friendly Spotify play-list, and if so, what would I put on it? Not everyone loves *The Greatest Showman* soundtrack (my unicorn mom friend does though!). If you can't tell, I was a wreck leading up to the playdate. When she finally got there, though, it was actually pretty great. We have the same sense of humor, we both watch period pieces, and we both love pop culture and gossip. We clicked. She wears Crocs and doesn't really drink, but I can let those things slide. She does seem to always have a charged phone, since she's really good at texting back at any hour. We both suffer from the affliction where you make plans with people but when the day of those plans comes, you pray that they cancel. The only problem with that is we never really hang out, because one of us is always canceling and the other is rejoicing. Even though we don't see each other a lot, we text all the time, so that's friendship, right?

It's tough out there for moms. Remember that pack of mothers who surrounded me and told me I needed to wear a Rolex to get my children into a fancy preschool? Not my people. And even if there were an app that allowed you to swipe right to match with mom friends, I don't think I would use it. I barely respond to my best friends and my family, so there is no way I'd be good at messaging and replying to strangers. It sounds exhausting. As I write this book, I'm just starting my life as a person who needs mom friends. I think it'll get easier when my kids are in elementary school and there are sports and things (right?!), but for now I am *trying* to battle my antisocial tendencies and get out there a little bit. I'm doing everything in my power to make a good impression. When I meet a new parent, I write their name and what they look like and what their kid's name is in my Notes app. It's my version of Anne Hathaway's giant book of photos and names that helps her help Meryl Streep remember who people are at the Met Gala in *The Devil Wears Prada*. I literally scroll through my Notes and try to memorize this shit! My Notes app looks like this:

Lucy Miller: Cody's mom, wears headbands, talked about puff jackets and kid-friendly restaurants

Micah Granger: Laurel's mom, owns a catering company, on a juice cleanse

Belinda Humphry: Olivia's mom, wears overalls, talked about baking

Serafina Zell: Preston's mom, interior designer, hates beige

What I'm looking for in friendships has changed since the early *Vanderpump* days. I'm still close with most of the friends I've made through the years, but priorities shift over time. How I am as a friend has changed too. I hope for the better. I spent my entire twenties being someone who was confrontational. I wasn't afraid to address anything in the moment and talk or argue (usually argue) wherever and whenever I felt like it. That was my MO.

Now? I'm tired. And therefore, more understanding. So instead of pouncing on things in the moment, I just sweep my feelings under the rug. I don't have the energy to argue, and any energy I do have I'd like to put toward things other than a mile-long text fight or a forty-five-minute call about a stupid conflict about who cheated or who called someone a bitch or who threw someone else under the bus. I'd rather just pretend the issue doesn't exist. I know any therapists reading this are probably horrified, but it's just how I operate now. Sweeping issues under the rug can be highly under-rated. Yes, I know it's *technically* best to acknowledge and express your feelings, but often, when I sweep something under the rug, I end up not being bothered by it anymore. I realize whatever the issue, it wasn't nearly as big of a deal as I thought it was. Sweeping it away gives me time to cool off.

All that said, Beau will definitely laugh when he reads this part of the book. To him and people close to me, I still express myself *maybe* a little too much when I feel something. I'm still a good arguer when I need to be, to the point that my family members are genuinely scared to get into a debate with me. I haven't had a lobotomy and completely changed my personality, but sometimes, a fight just isn't worth it, and a little rug sweep works for me.

I do think I'm failing a little bit as a friend, mainly because working and taking care of two kids takes up 7,098 hours that I used to spend on friendships. I know I need to put in more effort, but I can't do it all, right? I mean, can anyone? Replying to someone's text can derail my whole day! Maybe that's a little bit exaggerated, but the newborn phase is brutal, and then add a three-year-old to the mix, and forget it. I don't expect my friends to hit me up all the time anymore, so the friendships I cherish are the ones where we can go a long time without talking and then when we do see each other or talk, no one is bitter and we pick up like no time has passed. Basically I need low-maintenance friendships now, like my friendship with Taylor Strecker. If I were a lesbian, I would marry her, if she weren't already married. She's my female soul mate. I met her when I did her Sirius XM radio show after season one, and we both knew the minute we met that we were going to be friends. I could hang around her 24-7 and never get sick of her. We get each other's work ethic and sense of humor. It just clicks.

Most of the time if I am hanging out with a friend *and* my kids are around, I'm scatterbrained. Part of me is trying to communicate and have fun with my friend, and the other part has one eye on my kids to make sure they're still alive. It's simply how it is. "Having just enough" is the only way I know how to do friendship now. If a friend stops by for a few hours to hang out, that fills up my friendship tank for a long, long time.

I don't want to only have friends who are parents, but it is definitely nice to know someone who is pregnant at the same time as you are so you can text about aches and pains and swollen feet. If a friend doesn't have kids, it helps if they meet me a little more than halfway, since they don't have kids and school schedules and nap times. Jennifer Bush, who I met at SUR when we were little Hollywood club rats, was my first friend to ever have a baby. Now that I know what it's like to be a mom, I wish I could zip back in time and be there for her. She didn't have many friends with kids at that time, and us SUR girls didn't know the first thing about what she needed as a new mother. Jen happened to be pregnant (with her third) at the exact same time as I was pregnant with Messer. Our due dates were two days apart, and we were both having boys, so we reconnected and started texting about everything we were going through. Just to have someone to text about all the things we were going through took so much pressure off. We could commiserate together, or send links to each other for pregnancy dresses. I even caught her pregnancy craving. Is that a thing? Like the way girls can sync their periods? She told me she was craving peanut butter and jelly sandwiches, and from that day forward, all I could think about was raspberry jam. Seriously, my whole pregnancy was about when and how I could consume jam. Pregnancy can be so isolating, so just having someone text me that they were also having a midday brownie ice cream snack and that they too couldn't sleep at night made me feel less alone.

I also got to overlap for a few months with one of my best friends, Kristina Kelly. Her son is six months older than Messer. Kristina is the reason I started working at SUR. We met in the most basic way possible, during a night out in Hollywood. Back then I was all about bodycon Herve Leger–wannabe dresses with platform round-toe heels, false eyelashes, and statement necklaces (obvs). Les Deux was my favorite club, and then there was Goa, Hyde, Teddy's, the Roosevelt Hotel pool, Area, Opera . . . the list goes on. Before a night out clubbing, we would always meet up at someone's apartment ahead of time. We didn't have Uber or social media back then. All we had were taxis and BlackBerry messages. Any current twenty-four-year-old reading this probably thinks I am eight hundred years old. Whatever.

One night I was at a friend's apartment getting ready for a night out when she told me she had another friend coming who I'd never met. Someone knocked on the door, and for some reason I answered it even though it wasn't my apartment. I saw this chic tanned brunette girl in a white mini dress, leather jacket, and booties. I thought she was one of the chicest humans I had ever seen. She introduced herself, and I immediately blurted out how much I loved what she was wearing. And that's how Kristina and I became best friends. She was working at SUR at the time, and since I was always hanging out there, I figured I might as well start making money there, so she got me the job. If I had never met her, I would never have worked at SUR, which means I wouldn't have been on *Vanderpump*, which means I wouldn't have had the platform to start a podcast or write this book. We could even take it way further with this whole butterfly effect thing and say I wouldn't have met Beau, which means my children wouldn't exist if I hadn't met her. So basically, I owe it all to Kristina Kelly. Besides the fact that I owe MY LIFE to her, having our baby boys in the same year was ridiculously special. It was so helpful that she had just gone through everything I was experiencing, because I had somehow forgotten nearly everything about pregnancy and newborn life.

Instead of clubbing and wearing skintight dresses, I now prefer my friendships to involve pajamas and a text thread, or maybe a playdate, or—if we're lucky—brunch. One day I might have the motivation and time to plan a girls' trip again, but it will definitely not involve shared hotel rooms, 24-7 drinking, false eyelashes, drama, tears, and hangovers. If I were to get away for a weekend with friends now, each element of the trip would have to be planned and executed to perfection. If I'm going to take a few days away from my family and leave Beau with both kids, it better be good. I will 100 percent be splurging on a first-class flight, because a trip like this doesn't come around very often. I will absolutely not be sharing a room with anyone. I am surrounded by human beings around the clock, so Mama needs some alone time. Also, I'm just too old for that shit now.

The room will be a suite, because again, this sort of trip is very rare. The latest I would stay up would be midnight because I'm desperate for a full ten hours of sleep. I'd like to go the more civilized boozy dinner route so I don't have to waste a night of sleep on a hangover, which means we preferably eat before 8:00 p.m. I don't have the energy for false eyelashes anymore, so that's out. Also, as much as I would love to shop all day, I have kids to think about, so I can't go spending all my money on bags or shoes the way I used to. I know this may sound like I'm lacking in the fun department, but I'm always down for rosé all day! I just need to be in bed at a reasonable hour in a nice hotel room . . . by myself.

The Kinds of Moms You'll Meet

✳ **THE HOVERING MOM:** The hovering mom brings her kid to the park and acts as his shadow. She definitely gives me side-eye when she sees me scroll on my phone at a park bench, because apparently I too should be tracking my daughter's every move. God forbid she engages in some socializing or some independent play while I sit nearby. Hovering moms always make me feel like I'm a horrible mom if I'm not hovering too.

✳ **THE BREASTFEEDING MOM:** Before you breastfeeding moms get your panties in a twist because you see yourself on this list, just remember, I wish I were you. There is just something about a mom who breastfeed-ing has come easily to. They have this laid-back, go-with-the-flow, Mother Earth energy about them. They don't schedule feedings or naps, they don't stress about when the baby's last poop was. They love a good ethereal maxi dress with easy boob access. Breastfeeding moms just have a vibe about them.

SOME SORT OF FLOWER CROWN

OBVIOUSLY HER BABY IS IN A SLING

✳ **THE WINE MOM:** Doesn't matter what time or where. Kids' 10:00 a.m. birthday party at the park? She's got it covered with a mimosa in her personalized Yeti cup. She's got "mommy juice" and isn't afraid to poke fun at it. Parenting is hard, let the wine mom live.

✳ **THE MOM WHO TALKS LIKE THE YOUTUBE KIDS HOST MS. RACHEL:** You know the mom who always talks to her kids in that high-pitched voice, even if her kids are, like, fourteen? The one who is more famous than Jesus, at least to most toddlers? Yep, that one.

✳ **THE LORI LOUGHLIN MOM:** She's a wealth of knowledge when it comes to knowing which schools to get your kids into so that they can ultimately get into a better school to ultimately again get into an even better school. In fact, her kid's school is actually the only acceptable school. Your kid's school? Never heard of it. She has no problem donating a small house's worth of cash to get her kid into the school that will eventually get them an acceptance to Yale. It's an investment into her kid's future. The conversations are always school, school, school.

✳ **THE NO-SUGAR MOM:** I honestly get it, and I wish I would've started my parenting career as a no-sugar mom, because my daughter is solely motivated by sugar. Well, Elsa and sugar. I had this whole theory that if I were to keep Hartford away from sugar, that once she was around it, she'd act like a rabid dog to get her hands on it. Turns out, she was going to act like a rabid dog to get sugar regardless. So the no-sugar moms know what's up. And their kids are probably way healthier for it.

✳ **THE SCHEDULE-APP MOM:** It's me, hi, I'm the problem, it's me. I am 100 percent a schedule-app mom. This is normally a first-time mom thing, but in my case, my control-freak nature has prevailed and I am *still* a schedule-app mom. The second Hartford was born, I downloaded the Baby Connect app so I could track her sleep, eating, pooping, all of it. I'm not a go-with-the-flow mom who just feeds her babies when she senses they're hungry. I thrive with a schedule. I need to know my baby is going to nap for at least an hour at 9:00 a.m. or that he had three more ounces of formula than he did yesterday. My mom thinks my parenting style is absolutely insane, but a sane mom is a great mom, and knowing my baby's schedule keeps me sane.

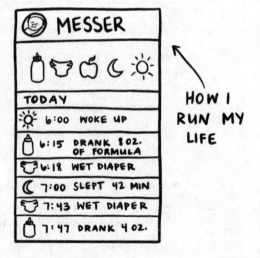

HOW I RUN MY LIFE

✳ **THE KNOW-IT-ALL MOM:** Know-it-all moms are really good at undercover mom-shaming. She's an expert on every illness, she's well-versed in baby milestones and why your baby isn't reaching one, and she is 100 percent judging you when your kid sneezes in a public place. They also tend to call themselves "baby whisperers," which is just code for "I'm better with babies than you are." Not all know-it-all moms are scary though; a lot of them just genuinely know a lot of shit about parenting. They read the books, they did the research, took one of the "Taking Cara Babies" courses.

✳ **THE COOL MOM:** Stylish, laid-back, makes her kid's Halloween costume herself, and has never used a generic birthday party invitation template, because naturally she designs her own. Her kids have a better wardrobe than I do, and she gets their snacks from the pricey cult supermarket Erewhon. She takes her kids to Coachella with their little pink oversize kid headphones, and they're in the VIP section, of course. She also probably surfs.

COOL MOM HOMEMADE TRUCK COSTUME

✳ **THE OVERSTEPPING MOM:** This is a two-parter. Some backstory first: Before Hartford started going to school, our nanny, Sonia, would take her to our neighborhood park every day while we worked. So whenever I took her to the park on a random weekend day, I'd run into moms who would make a show of it and say, "Oh, wow, look who came to the park today," like I'm some absentee parent who doesn't spend time with my kid. Bonus points for when those moms act like they're your kid's bestie when you run into them. Like they see each other soooooo often without you to the point where it makes you feel like the odd man out with your own child.

Making friends when you're five or fifteen or twenty-five might seem tough, but making mom friends is BRUTAL. Maybe not always, but you're forced together not because you have so much in common but because you both have tiny humans to care for and you're tired. As a parent, you don't need three or five or fifteen friends to go out with. You need one or two unicorn mom or dad friends to text or see occasionally, just to feel human. Don't feel like you're failing if you only have half a mom friend. That's something! A neighbor you hang out with once a season? Great! A school mom you talk to at Valentine's Day parties? You're doing great.

CHAPTER 10

The (Im)Perfect Wife

You know those magical early days of falling in love, when you're both just floating along in a bubble of bliss and sex and you're still laughing at each other's jokes? Like, for-real laughing, not pretend laughing just so you don't hurt the other person's feelings? I mean, my husband makes me laugh, but no one is hilarious 24-7 and 365 days a year. (Except maybe Will Ferrell. Nothing is funnier to me than the movie *Step Brothers*.)

When Beau and I started falling for each other, we would spend almost every night drinking wine, exchanging stories, listening to music and dancing in my kitchen. We would play Pitbull, Robyn, Bob Marley, Kygo, Kesha. Beau really broke me out of my full-on show tunes addiction and inspired me to listen to other music, but I will *never* abandon Broadway. We wanted to be around each other so much that sleeping would've been an interruption. So we spent countless nights flirting and getting to know each other, without a care in the world. Well, maybe one care, which was that the love we were feeling would last forever. That was pretty much it though.

I remember one specific night when we had just become "official" in our relationship, after we exchanged *I love you*s for the first time. On that night, Beau said something that I still think about on a regular basis. When he said it, we were dancing around my apartment. Before you choke on our cuteness, just know that I'm a horrible dancer. This was not like *La La Land*–esque choreographed dancing beneath moonlight in the Hollywood Hills. Beau did teach elderly people ballroom dancing, so *he* had moves, but he has been trying to teach me ever since we met. It has been seven years and I still suck, mind you. His elderly students were good though! Maybe when I'm eighty-two, his guidance will finally sink in.

Anyway, while he was waltzing and I was moving around like Elaine from *Seinfeld*, he looked at me and said, "I hope for the rest of our lives we still do this. I hope we'll always dance around our kitchen at night." He must have *really* loved me, because like I said, I am not at my best when I'm dancing.

That night was one of the sweetest and most important moments in our relationship, because what he meant was that he wanted to spend the rest of his life with me. It was also such a hopeful moment, because at the time, I truly believed that we would always be so head-over-heels in love that regardless of what life would bring, we'd always still spend our nights dancing in the kitchen. Ahhh, young(ish) love. It feels like there are zero responsibilities, that you two are the only people in the world, and it will be like that forever. I think about that moment often, because now we definitely do not spend every night drinking and dancing and making out in our kitchen. I always feel a little guilty because I know if I asked him to dance with me in the kitchen after we put our kids down, it would make his day, month, and year. But life is busy, work gets stressful, we have two children who demand so much of our energy and time, that by the end of the day, I am talked out, touched out—basically any "out" you can think of, that's me. Very often I feel like I'm just not nailing it as a wife. But what does nailing it as a wife even mean? Bringing your spouse a homemade pot roast after a hard day? Putting on lace lingerie after you've changed 425 diapers and your face has been smeared with smashed peas? Please. Beau *deserves* to have someone dance with him every night, but Mama's tired.

One Tuesday night pretty soon after Messer was born, we were listening to music in the kitchen and Beau was cleaning the dishes. That's his usual move after he puts Hartford to bed. I had just washed my face and finished my skin-care routine, which is *my* usual move after I put Messer down. Alexa was playing the *Encanto* soundtrack (don't judge), and I guess I was feeling nostalgic (or ambitious), so I brought up our late-night dancing era. Beau got all excited. Whoops. He said, "We can dance right now!" I didn't want to be the worst wife in the world, so I got up and summoned every bit of energy I had left, which was not much, and we spent a good ninety seconds soberly dancing to "Colombia, Mi Encanto" in our kitchen. My shirt was covered in baby spit-up, so it was not the sexy vibe either of us remembered. At least we tried though.

If you're not married, you might think our ninety-second spit-up dance means our romance is dead. If you *are* married and have kids, you might think our ninety-second spit-up dance is crazy romantic and you can't even fathom how I had the energy to move my feet at *all* past 8:00 p.m. and WTF, I am the *best* wife in the world. I think the answer is somewhere in between. I'm not going to lie, it has been way harder to make time for each other since having our second baby, but we do try, and that's what matters. After both the kids are finally down for bed, we'll ask each other, "Do you want to hang out? Do you want to talk? Do you want to watch something together?" Most nights we do one of those things. But then there are nights where either one or both of us just need alone time and we do our own thing in our house. He'll go build a LEGO spaceship or Viking village in his gentleman's library while he watches some sort of *Star Wars* spin-off show, and I'll go take a shower, spend extra time on my skin-care routine, maybe self-tan a little, do my nails and watch a historical drama series like *The Serpent Queen.* I know it's healthy to have alone time, but I still always feel a little guilty that I'm not being the best partner I can be. He's still my favorite person to be around, but it's hard to switch into "cool, fun girlfriend" mode when you've already spent the day working and parenting together. Isn't it crazy that once you find yourself in a safe, stable, healthy relationship, that's when you stop doing things that made you love that safe, stable relationship in the first place? I have never felt more taken care of, more secure with someone . . . and now I drop the ball? But also why do we put pressure on ourselves to be a perfect partner when we are TIRED?

Here's the thing. It's harder to find the time or energy to be romantic after a second kid because now neither of us can tap out. With Hartford, yes it was hard and it tested our relationship, but we had a rhythm going and we could take turns, so neither of us got too burned out. Now there is zero tapping out, ever. There are two of them and two of us and one of us has to keep the baby from rolling down the stairs while the other makes sure Hartford isn't drawing red squiggles on the wall with a marker. We're like two ships passing in the night sometimes. We have to work on communicating and being friends and lovers. Also, if I'm especially tapped out, I have a tendency to go rogue and pick fights. Some nights after we put the babies down, instead of saying, "Hey, honey, let's dance!" I'm like: "Why aren't you trying to have a conversation with me?! You don't even care! I spent nine months sacrificing my body and my mind for this baby and now it's your turn to pick up the slack and go above and beyond!" It's not a good seduction technique.

I've asked some of my friends with kids when Beau and I will get back to normal again, and their answer is always "In a few years?"

That's depressing as shit! I mean, I get it—once your kids are able to entertain each other, maybe then you get to start spending more time with your partner again? So yeah, three years sounds about right. Beau is one of the best things to ever happen to me. There isn't a day that goes by that I don't recognize how lucky I am that he's my husband. He's funny, smart; his moral compass is better than anyone else I know; he's handsome. I always tell him he has the best gladiator legs. He's an incredible father, and he quite literally has never disrespected me or even raised his voice at me. I could not love him more, but I do a shitty job of showing it sometimes because the stresses of life squeeze out any ounce of energy I have.

When we do get away, it's usually an hour-and-a-half lunch when Hartford is at school and Messer is with the nanny. We hurry to a restaurant close to the house, order, and then we sit in silence because we both need to decompress so badly. Then we realize we are sitting in silence and we laugh and talk about the kids for forty-five minutes. Maybe we need to carry around a bullet-point list of topics for those moments so we can have conversations about travel or books or philosophy. For real though, I think both of us would rather just talk about our kids. They're cute and sweet and we made them!

I don't know how it works with C-section births, but six weeks after a vaginal birth, you go to your doctor, they examine you, and give you the okay to go jogging or ride a bike or have sex. It's a little bit weird to go from feeling like your uterus is going to fall out of your body to hearing, "Everything looks great, you can have sex now!" Like, are you SURE? Did you maybe miss something down there? I am not proud of this, but I am trying to be real with y'all: I actually contemplated having my doctor write me a note saying I was not ready to have sex yet. I brought it up with him, and instead of being scandalized he said, "You're not the first person to ask me that." So you all are doing it too! I feel so guilty, but when I am pregnant and right after childbirth I am just not in the mood for sex five times a day (or week). Once a week? Twice a week? Yes! That wouldn't be a problem if I didn't have a husband who was in the mood seven days a week.

When I'm pregnant I feel like some sort of wild beast that smells and roots around in the dirt all day. I could be wearing a chic monochromatic pregnancy outfit and have my makeup and hair done, but trust me, I feel like Quasimodo from *The Hunchback of Notre Dame*. During those times, if Beau's leg even grazes mine on accident I'm like, "NO!" I feel like a creature from *The Hills Have Eyes*. Some might say I look like Gollum's long lost cousin, or that if *Star Wars* were real, my 23andMe results would link me directly to Jabba the Hutt. We don't acknowledge that there is crazy shit going on with our bodies when we have kids. Your hormones are running wild, you don't feel like yourself, but yet we're supposed to *pretend* like we feel just fine. Yes, some women are like, *I feel so beautiful when I'm pregnant and also when I am giving birth naturally at our farmhouse*, but come on! So many of us do not feel like a goddess of fertility during those times; we feel like a gorgon, and not the hot Medusa type of gorgon. I always try to remember to take a breath and remind myself that we will get back to having more consistent romance. Maybe not dancing in the kitchen every night, but I won't have the urge to get a doctor's note to excuse me from sex.

Before Messer was conceived, Beau and I took a trip to Las Vegas. We'd been back there with Hartford, but we hadn't been there as a couple since we filmed a Vegas trip for *Vanderpump*. And yes, I know you know that I Dark Passenger–ed on that first trip. This time, we were walking to Caesars Palace and saw a sign for a live show called *Absinthe*, which reminded me of one of the biggest fights Beau and I had ever gotten into. So I looked over at Beau, and said, "Maybe, for old time's sake, I should role-play and Dark Passenger you on this trip." He was like, no, thank you. But I was serious! Like maybe we needed to ignite a little passion and get crazy and maybe if I felt like he was on the verge of divorcing me it would spice things up, kind of like the way makeup sex can spice things up? I thought it sounded like a good idea, but he was horrified. Anyway, I'm pretty sure Messer was conceived on that trip, so something must have worked.

After nine months of pregnancy and about a month of newborn life after Messer was born, Beau and I mustered the collective energy to create our costumes for Halloween 2023. Halloween brings out the best in me. So we decided to dress in the theme Edgar Allan Beau: Beau was Edgar Allan Poe, and the kids and I were ravens. You know, like the poem. Anyway, Edgar Allan Poe lived in the 1800s and mustaches were hip, I guess, so Beau shaved his facial hair into a mustache, because when we decide on Halloween costumes, we commit. I loved our theme, but I am not a mustache girlie. In fact, I *hate* a mustache. So of course Beau loved it, and he got so excited about this new look and said he can keep it for another month in honor of Movember, when men grow these disgusting things to raise awareness for men's health. Like, can't they just wear a rubber bracelet or green shoes for a month instead? Anything but a freaking mustache. When Beau told me he was keeping the thing, I blurted, "Absolutely not. If you ever want to be romantic with me again, you'll get rid of it when the clock strikes midnight on Halloween."

| ACCEPTABLE MUSTACHES | UNACCEPTABLE MUSTACHES |

FOR COSTUMES BECAUSE WE COMMIT!

HOW CAN I EVEN FIND YOUR LIPS

OVER AMBITIOUS HIPSTER

REALLY JUST A WALRUS

FRENCH WAITER OR SERIAL KILLER

*TRICK QUESTION. ALL MUSTACHES ARE ICK.

I guess he didn't take my direct, blunt reaction seriously, because for the next few days he walked around the house with *that thing* on his face. Because of this, I was in a horrible mood. Every time he tried to ask me a question about work or the kids, I snapped at him. I felt like I was living with some kind of kidnapper. There's just something unsavory about a strip of hair above a man's lip. It says I HAVE A FAMILY TIED UP IN THE BASEMENT or I LIKE TO MAIM PEOPLE. Mustaches just make me think of sinister things. I don't want to start thinking my husband is harboring gross secrets. So after a few days of picking fights and trying to live with this thing, I lost it.

"That mustache is a slap in the face! It means you don't care what I think or feel. You don't care if I find you attractive. I make an effort to put on makeup and try to look pretty! You don't respect me or our relationship!"

Maybe I took it a little too far, but I was desperate. Beau left the room and took a break so we could cool down, which is a healthy response to conflict that he learned from his therapist mom, which sometimes pisses me off even though it's 100 percent the right thing to do. After his break he came back into the room and said he'd shave it, which made me so happy. I quietly vowed to never allow a Halloween costume that involved weird facial hair ever again.

The night after our fight, I looked over at Beau before bed and said, "Oh my god, you shaved it!" I thought I was being all supportive and that this would be a moment of love and connection between us. Maybe we would even have sex!

"Are you fucking kidding me right now?" he said, clearly hurt.

"What?"

"I shaved it this morning. You didn't notice for a full day. Now *my* feelings are hurt because it's like you don't even truly look at me or see me."

I felt so guilty. This freaking mustache! I had made such a big deal about it and caused a big fight, and then I didn't even notice when it was gone. We are in the same house 24-7, we work and parent together within the same walls. How had I not noticed? It broke my heart a little bit. I felt so mean. We didn't sit down and discuss what happened because we were too tired. We just moved on. I guess the moral of the story is that no one is perfect in marriage, and what seems like a small thing to you can mean a lot to the other person.

I am not trying to make it sound like relationships or marriages all implode as soon as you have a kid. For all our hard days, we have so many more good moments, but this isn't a book that's about showing only the good moments. It's a book about being honest about the harder moments. Like so many things, there's just this insane amount of pressure to be good at it all—to be a great mom and also well-rested and sexy and a hard worker and romantic and attentive and responsible. It's a lot. Yes, I hate a mustache, but even though I don't like sports, I'll support my husband and his LA Rams obsession by allowing our kids to wear Rams gear, or (occasionally) going to a football game with him. I like hot dogs and beer and tailgating, but it's always such a production to get to the stadium, and then get concessions, and then find your seats. And why are there so many innings or quarters or whatever? I hate having to bring a clear purse (gross), but I will do it for love, sometimes, if he really, really begs me to go. I support him in his Rams journey, even though I find it boring AF. This is called meeting your partner halfway. Beau meets me halfway or more than halfway every single day, because I get to be in charge.

It's almost laughable when I hear our podcast episodes from before we had kids, when I was still on *Vanderpump* and we were totally blissed out. People would ask us the secrets to a happy relationship, but no one should be giving advice when they're still in the early stages of love. I want advice from people who've been married for fifty years. Like here I am now, and I can barely get it together enough to flirt with my husband. *That's* real shit! One thing Beau and I wholeheartedly agree on is that we will always make an effort to be a couple that tries to put our relationship first, before the kids even. That might sound polarizing, but if we're not in sync and happy, how can we be the best versions of ourselves for the kids? That said, we're in this temporary phase of newborn and toddler life where it's more about surviving each day, but we're doing it together. I know one day, maybe even by the time you read this, we will have gotten away for an actual vacation as a couple. Hopefully by the time you are holding this book in your hands, Beau and I will be laughing about how worried we were that we'd never have time for each other again.

When you look at celebrity couples like Blake Lively and Ryan Reynolds, it seems like they are happy and content ALL THE TIME. They walk around New York in their winter coats arm in arm, laughing. They have four children but they still flirt with each other via Instagram. They seem like a solid, awesome couple, so they are my goals celebrity couple, even though I am sure they argue and have their moments. They have FOUR KIDS. Beau is still the person I want to talk to, to share things with. I'm just in a phase where I'm overwhelmed and tired; therefore, not as exciting as I used to be. But hey, awareness is the first step to making a change, right? It helps if you try to figure out what each other's love language is, as cheesy as that might sound. Beau's love language is acts of service, because he does things for me all day. He'll make meals or bring me coffee. I am more about quality time. I had previously thought physical touch was my love language because the ex-boyfriend who shall only be referred to as Manbun used to withhold touch as punishment. Once we were over a fight, if he put his arm around me, I'd feel this wave of relief. It was sadistic, and he was just torturing and manipulating me. So another piece of advice is: Don't marry the person who treats you like crap! You're welcome.

If you're not married or in a relationship, do me a favor: Enjoy your single years! I look back at the freedom and independence I had to travel or buy things or do embarrassing things in my apartment . . . like post videos of myself crying over Manbun. But seriously, being alone is underrated. It can be quite a beautiful life, and if you embrace being alone, settling becomes less probable. If you're single, you could change your life tomorrow in any way you want, but once you're in a committed relationship with kids you can't just do that unless you pull a *Gone Girl* and disappear to a roadside motel. You can have a fulfilling, amazing life doing whatever you want, and if that's your journey, embrace the shit out of it. Think of it this way: if you're single, you aren't subjected to dad jokes. I swear, a guy can be an award-winning stand-up comedian, but as soon as he has kids, the dad jokes just start coming out of his mouth. It's like they can't help it.

So after all the ups and downs and fights and makeups, I still really love my relationship. That doesn't mean it's always easy! There was a TikTok trend where people shared part of a scene from *Euphoria* where the boyfriend and girlfriend pass each other in a hallway and don't even acknowledge each other, and they'd add comments like "Me and my husband after having kids." If you *believe* that trend, it would probably scare the shit out of you and prevent you from ever having kids. When I saw it, it made me feel lucky that I didn't resent Beau. It was just such a dark and negative view, like it was a fearmongering ad trying to scare the shit out of pregnant women. Yes, I am not on my A game in the flirting/seducing/being the perfect partner department, but my relationship isn't falling apart. It's natural for things to shift and change. It can actually get better, but in different ways. It's a different type of love; it's become deeper, more forgiving, safer and more fulfilling. It feels like true, seasoned, committed love. One night I was lamenting the fact *The Buccaneers* and *The Gilded Age* finales were happening during the same week, and I wouldn't have another period piece to watch. As I was getting ready for bed, I got a text from Beau. It was a link to an article titled "18 Best Period Dramas to Watch for *The Crown* and *Bridgerton* Fans." It's simple, but that's love.

More consistent romance *will* come back. I can embrace the dad jokes and baby spit-up dance sessions and exhaustion. What I cannot embrace, not ever again, is a mustache.

Takeaway

Love is not dancing on rooftops as an orchestra that your lover paid for plays down below. I mean, that's not *NOT* love, but it's not realistic, day-in-and-day-out, we-are-in-this-together love. Marriage is hard, but it can also be great. Those nights of dancing in the kitchen might not happen as often, but when they do, they're even more special than they were in the days before kids and a mortgage and trash days came along. You can have it all in love and marriage, but not 24-7, 365 days a year. And that's fine! Love is not about having it all, it's about loving each other, *even* if one of you grows a mustache.

CHAPTER 11

The Show Must Go On . . . Even When You're Pregnant, Sober, and Unsure Whether or Not Anyone Will Buy a Ticket

usical theater is in my blood. Not because five generations of my family have been stars of the Broadway stage or anything, but because I just freaking love show tunes and drama and people who emote onstage as if their lives depended on it. I had an entire chapter devoted to show tunes in my first book called "Why Musical Theater Is Cool AF." There is just so much to love about it, and it makes me feel good. I lean into the things that make me feel joy, and "One Day More" from *Les Mis* is freaking joyous.

My 2019 *Straight Up with Stassi* podcast tour was kind of like my version of musical theater. I had a bejeweled microphone, stage sets, a tour manager, a four-person crew, and a rider (more on that later). It was glorious, until it wasn't. The tour ended, the world shut down, and I was confined to my cell/home like everyone else. Back in 2020, if you had told me I'd get a second chance to do another *Straight Up with Stassi* tour, I would have thought you were unhinged and on eight thousand drugs. But then one day, a miracle happened. Or, I accidentally set a miracle into motion.

By January 2023, I'd gotten back on my feet work-wise. I was doing the podcast again, I had agents, and one day I was on a call with those agents. We were going through updates about various things I was working on, and once I'd talked about those things, I felt bad that the tour agent was getting nothing from me. So out of embarrassment, or some kind of guilt-panic, I blurted, "Also—I'm ready to tour again!"

I was not ready to tour again. At all.

First of all, it takes a lot to put on a tour. Yes it's time and effort and energy, but also . . . money. Lots of it. During the first tour, I had that *Vanderpump* money coming in, so I paid a tour manager and they were like, "You can do whatever you want! Pyrotechnics or giant disco balls! A live elephant onstage? Why not!" At first I was giddy, thinking I could just create my very own *Phantom of the Opera* meets *Chelsea Lately* (RIP) extravaganza. Then I realized that I would now be paying for all those disco balls and fireworks. If I wanted a big Daenerys Targaryen entrance moment, it was coming out of my pocket. I didn't go *crazy* with the budget during that first tour, but we did pay a tour manager and a crew who traveled with us. We had a whole stage set of furniture that was supposed to mimic my actual living room, which required giant moving trucks hauling that furniture from city to city. I paid a stand-up comedy writer to help me with my set. I thought that was the only way to do it.

So when my new agents started encouraging me to do another tour, I put off the decision for weeks, even though I had (accidentally) suggested it. I was afraid of coming back from my rock bottom/no career/opposite-of-a-girlboss era and putting on a subpar show with bad sound, lame sets, and zero bedazzlement. No one was going to pay money to see me stand on a bare stage and ramble, sober and pregnant. People want pizzazz! There was no way I could go on a half-ass follow-up tour.

But then, just like scaling my wedding down or turning my beautiful closet into Messer's nursery, I eventually realized that scaling down the tour didn't mean I wasn't having or giving the full experience. It just meant it would be different. Maybe . . . it could even be better?

For the 2023 tour, instead of having a crew and furniture to mimic my actual apartment and disco balls, we thought simpler. We paid our friend and assistant Lo to be the tour manager. Lo started out as my assistant seven years ago, and she's my manager and right-hand woman in everything I do. I like to say if I'm the CEO, she's the COLo. So it was just me, Beau, Lo, and Taylor Strecker, who had also been on the first tour. Our set was simple, and I used the same bedazzled mics we used on the first tour. We projected photos and graphics of my family, Taylor, and things and people I like, like Meghan Markle, *Outlander*, *Medici*, and Marie Antoinette, onto the wall behind us. I wanted the backdrop to be like Hogwarts, where all the paintings move. Everything else (chairs, table, rug) was provided by each theater. We settled on the theme of "The Mommy Dearest Tour," since I was pregnant and and the 1981 movie *Mommie Dearest* with Faye Dunaway as Joan Crawford scares the shit out of me. It just felt like the right vibe, and I knew I could make something out of that theme. We set our dates and cities, and Lo handled logistics and even learned how to use a professional program that's used for visuals, lighting, and sound levels for a stage. Instead of paying someone to write my set, I took a pen and notebook, got into my bed one day, and wrote some stand-up and dialogue in a day. I was so proud of myself, taking on this thing that I thought I needed help with before. But I'm not a comedian, and getting onstage sober and pregnant and trying to make people laugh seemed terrifying. When we told people we were going on the road with no experienced tour manager and no crew, you would have thought I'd proclaimed I was running for president and that I'd be doing my own campaign.

But sometimes, you think you need more—more money, more help, more glitter—but what you do with limited resources, on your own, may actually turn out better.

When we were in Minneapolis for our first show at the Pantages Theatre, this beautiful, historic place that opened in 1916, I remember rehearsing with Beau and Taylor and feeling so nervous that I might actually puke. On the previous tour, we could power our confidence and soothe our nerves with many, many Aperol spritzes, but this time around, I just had to sit with the nerves and deal with any anxieties that popped up. I remember each of us went to a different corner of the hotel room to practice our lines, which I hate doing anyway. I don't like to rehearse telling jokes too much since it can stifle the spontaneity. When we came back together, we were all like, "There is no way we will remember all of this."

"What if my mind just goes blank in the middle of this big historic theater?" I asked.

"You're a podcast host, you won't forget," Taylor said.

"I'm not sure about that."

So nerves and all, we ate pizza and then went out onto the bare-bones stage to face an audience that had paid for tickets and dressed up and came out to be entertained. We didn't forget our bits, and the audience laughed in all the right moments, and we had a blast. When we went back into the greenroom after the show, there was this collective feeling of: *Did we? But how? But we did that. . . .* It was such a great feeling. We pulled it off, without all the bells and whistles. That was just the first stop though. We had many more to go.

Almost everything on that tour taught me to lean into "you can't have it all, but maybe what you get will be better" energy. We had so many canceled flights, but then we'd end up taking a four-hour train ride and I discovered that I love train trips. It makes me feel like I'm living my best European vacation lifestyle, just looking out the window at the towns whizzing by. I also missed Hartford, which was tough, and I had plenty of guilt being away from her. I loved the days we'd get to take a break and go home to just be with her. Some shows were harder than others. Ask any performer and they'll tell you that New York City is one of the most stressful places to have a show. Maybe Patti LuPone and Lin-Manuel Miranda don't get nervous, but *most* people do. New York means there are industry people and agents and managers. On our first tour, I gripped the Swarovski crystal–encrusted microphone so hard from nerves that I had indentations on my palms for like an hour after the NYC show. Even when I told my brain to relax my hand, I could not do it. We got through it though and headed to the next town.

If Minneapolis felt amazing and New York was stressful, well, Milwaukee was . . . testy.

I love going to Milwaukee because we stay in this insanely beautiful haunted hotel called the Pfister, which opened in 1893. It has a Victorian art collection, which I am all about. So with the history and splendor and Victorian vibes, it was a little surprising to exit the elevator at night after our show ended and see hundreds of professional dancers dressed in feathers and skimpy outfits with their tanned six-pack abs and perfect perky boobs on full display. There I was, pregnant and feeling like Shrek, and there they were, these cellulite-free, tan, glowy dancers practicing their high kicks. We got to our room, and I was feeling so gross, I just wanted to eat room service and crawl under the covers. Beau had other ideas. When we were having dinner he kept suggesting that we go watch the dance competition, and I was like there is not a cell in my being that wants to go watch human Barbie dolls in their tiny *Dancing with the Stars*–esque costumes kicking their long perfect legs to the sky at ten o'clock at night. I could barely hoist my swollen legs onto the bed. Beau kept asking, which only made me more moody and more angry. We don't fight often, but that dance competition was not a highlight of the tour. Basically, I told Beau he could go watch the dancers over my pissed-off, hormonal dead body. I totally spiraled, thinking of him out there watching the hottest girls in Milwaukee while I beached myself in our hotel bed and ate leftover pizza. Anyway, no one saw the dance competition that night.

Despite that little hiccup, I loved and will always love going to Milwaukee because of that hotel and the theater we performed in, the Pabst. It's—you guessed it—historic and lavish. It's the kind of place I imagine Lincoln being assassinated in, a place presidents and princesses visited. Not every theater is a dream though. There was a place we booked that looked like a weird apartment complex where a therapist would rent an apartment for their practice. It didn't feel like a theater at all. The greenroom was like the *Saw* basement, and it was by far the tiniest space we'd performed in. I was nervous at first, but when we went out I ended up making a joke about it being kind of a weird place, and the audience ended up being one of the most enthusiastic, cool audiences of the whole tour. So don't judge a theater by the gleam of its chandeliers (or its total lack of chandeliers). I mean, maybe I'll judge the theater, but never again will I judge the audience.

Speaking of judging. Maybe you remember all the gossip years ago about one diva who requested everything in the greenroom be white? Or that some musician or actor demanded a bowl of only green M&M'S, which means that some theater or club employee has to pick out all the tiny green M&M'S and put them in a bowl? Growing up, I remember reading these things and associating it with diva behavior. Well, these requests come on what's called a rider, which is basically a list of the food and drinks and whatever else a performer wants in the dressing room. I've always found riders super embarrassing and borderline cringe, even though it is lovely to have the things you want to eat or drink waiting for you before a show. I have a love/hate relationship with these lists, but they are a very normal part of touring. Still, it can feel a little asshole-ish to ask for a bottle of Hidden Valley ranch at every tour stop, which I do. I mean, I like to order pizzas when we're hanging out backstage before the show and not every pizza place stocks ranch!

On our second tour, Lo asked me to fill out my rider. Of course I asked for my ranch, plus some snacks and sparkling water, and we added wine or beers or whatever Beau and Taylor wanted. I was so insecure about my ranch request that when we met the managers and employees at each theater, the first thing I said to them after saying hello was, "I just want you to know that I don't drink ranch dressing straight from the bottle. It's for pizza." They usually responded by saying, "Yeah, we thought that was weird to have ranch and no food to eat it with."

Before we left for the tour, Lo kept encouraging me to add

more things to my rider. Deep down I wanted to add more things, but I also didn't want to be an asshole. She said that it's very normal to have a long list and that theater managers expect it. It was a constant battle between me being embarrassed and me just accepting the fact that having a robust rider does not mean you are a raging egomaniac. But then, the photo appeared.

About halfway through the tour, we walked into the greenroom to find our little table of snacks and drinks. Then I saw that there was a framed picture of my hero, Marie Antoinette. Huh. I was like, "That's such a good sign. This show is going to be good, I just know it. I mean what are the odds of a random picture of Marie Antoinette being here at this theater in Dallas?"

"Oh, we put that in the rider," Lo said.

Excuse me, but WHAT?! So of course I lost my shit. Lo explained that the production team suggested that you put something really random and specific on your list so you know the theater employees read the whole thing. I mean. MARIE ANTOI-NETTE! If it ever got out that I had actually requested at every tour stop a picture of an eighteenth-century French queen who supposedly had a clothing allowance of $20,000 *per day* in today's dollars, people would crucify me.

SUNS The Mommy Dearest Tour 2023
Technical and Hospitality Rider

Hospitality:

Any cuts must be approved by "The Mommy Dearest Tour" Tour Manager prior to engagement.

Portable Ice—refilled as needed—**lots of it! Please have available at "artist arrival."**

Plates, glasses, napkins, silverware for 4 people

1x 6-pack of orange sparkling Celcius (sub: sugar-free Red Bull)

1x bottle of Sancerre wine

1x bottle of prosecco

1x bottle of Aperol

1x small bottle of Teremana tequila (sub: Casamigos tequila)

12-pack of Miller Lite

12-pack of Diet Coke

12-pack of Pellegrino sparkling water

4x Snapple peach tea ZERO sugar (glass or plastic bottles)

4x Tejava bottles unsweetened (sub: Gold Peak unsweetened)

1x 64 oz. bottle of 100 percent cranberry juice (must be sweetened Ocean Spray)

10x limes with knife and cutting board

1x bottle of Hidden Valley ranch dressing

1x 16 oz. bag of teriyaki-flavored beef jerky

1x 6–8 oz. bag of Goldfish (original flavor with no artificial flavors or preservatives—blue package)

6-pack of muffins from grocery store bakery (e.g. blueberry, banana, apple—no lemon or chocolate please)

1x bag of family size (18 oz.) mini Snickers

1x bag of family size (18 oz.) Reese's Pieces

12-pack Handisnacks dippers (Premium Breadsticks and Cheese or Ritz Crackers and Cheese)

1x bottle of hand sanitizer with pump (8 oz.)

1x framed photo of any version of Marie Antoinette, set up in the main dressing room

"We put in there that it could be any photo they liked," Lo said, trying to make me feel better about it. She had it added to the rider halfway through the tour, and somehow I hadn't noticed any of the other whatever-photo-you-like Marie Antoinette pictures. There was nothing I could do about it at that point, since removing things and adding things to a rider is a major hassle. You have to go through like five people at each theater. It's way too much work. Actually, I confess, once I accepted the fact that this totally unnecessary and ridiculous item was on my rider, I came to love it. My basic bitch self leaned in to it, and it made me feel like each room was personalized, or like I had a little piece of home with me. Basically, it was the equivalent of some people's Virgin Mary photos. It brought me comfort.

The last stop of the Mommy Dearest Tour was back home in Los Angeles. At first, I didn't even want to do an LA show because it's almost worse than New York. There are the agents and industry people again, plus everyone in LA is so jaded. At least people in Manhattan are enthusiastic. The more I thought about it though, I realized that it was our hometown show, and we could do it on my birthday since I had no plans. We found a beautiful theater at the Ace Hotel downtown, and I thought we could bring Hartford out onstage, which would be so sweet, especially since we'd been away from her on and off to go do this tour. We had a disco ball, a fog machine, and we had a backdrop from the movie *Frozen*, so she could go out there and live her best Elsa life. If you know anything about toddlers, you know that this was either a great plan or the absolute worst plan two parents had ever hatched. She could go out there and love the stage, or she could totally melt down in a way that would make it look like we were two LA parents forcing their small child into the spotlight.

I'd seen her at her dance recital and she'd had zero stage fright, so that gave me a little confidence. The day of the show we brought Hartford to the theater early and let her walk around the stage to get used to it. Instead of stressing about it and hoping for a perfect outcome, I just had to trust that we'd had a great tour, and that this would hopefully be an even greater ending.

When Hartford walked out, she was all about that spotlight (thank God). She held a microphone and belted out "Let It Go," or at least the words she knew from "Let It Go." She was dancing around and waving at the audience. It was the cutest freaking thing. She loved it so much that Beau had to throw her over a shoulder and haul her offstage as she yelled, "Nooooooo!" It was such a fun and perfect way to end a tour that I wasn't even sure we could pull off, and it's now a core memory that I will cherish forever. And we didn't need a professional tour manager, a massive set, or pyrotechnics to make it work.

Takeaway

I was so afraid that people would just want the season-one or season-four Stassi on a podcast tour and that they'd be bored by this new version of myself where I was pregnant and not toting around a cocktail. But then I realized that I don't have to remain the same psychopathic, backhanding, drink-slinging person I was before. Everyone is growing together and aging at the same time. It makes me feel more comfortable in my career. No one wants to see the same thing over and over again, whether it's you or me. Basically, be yourself, even if you're scared no one will accept it. I promise, someone somewhere will.

CHAPTER 12

The Dark Passenger
Is No Joke

Back in the *Next Level Basic* days, I wrote about "self-care Sundays," and doing things to treat myself, like having spa days and colonics. Nowadays if I ever have a few hours to myself to chill and focus on wellness, there is no way in hell I will spend that time getting a colonic. Even a fancy Los Angeles colonic where they give you champagne afterward. If I get a few precious hours alone, hours that I don't have to think about another human being, you will find me luxuriating in a twenty-minute soothing face mask and drinking a glass of even more soothing wine, at home. There is no such thing as "self-care Sundays" anymore, but there is "self-care for one hour on Tuesday when the kids go to bed" time. I take full advantage of those fleeting moments.

It's important to take time for yourself no matter what stage of life you're in, but there's a whole new meaning to self-care for me now—yet I'm still failing at it a bit. Just like when we put pressure on ourselves to kill it at work or as a parent or as a friend, there is actually pressure to be serene and find time for wellness. Isn't it kind of messed up that we stress if we don't get enough wellness time? If you're not making turmeric smoothies and syncing your sleep cycle to the rhythms of nature (it's a thing), then you're failing at . . . what? At relaxation? Health? Indulgence? If you've synced your sleep cycle to the moon, then good for you. Maybe one day I'll experience enough sleep FOMO that I'll become desperate to try it. Until then, I am also failing at sleep.

Like most things, when it comes to mental health, it's not just about me anymore. If I don't prioritize that now, I'm a bad mom. My kids' lives depend on me staying happy and (semi)balanced. How I act and feel affects two innocent human beings, so the stakes are way higher now than they were when it was me on *Vander-pump*, losing my shit at a party. If I took this conversation seriously before, I take it a million times more seriously now. I'm not talking about massages and facial steams, I'm talking about actual psycho-logical well-being. I should 100 percent be in therapy right now, because I know it helps me feel less anxious. Am I in therapy? No. Why? Because I don't have that many free hours, and it seems like a daunting task that would take up so much time just to try and find a therapist I actually like. Basically . . . I'm working on it.

In the past, I've talked about my respect for/obsession with people like Meghan Markle or Marie Antoinette, but never in a million years would I have thought there would come a time where I would cite David Beckham as a personal idol of mine. Victoria Beckham? Yes. But David? He's handsome and looks good in tighty-whities, but besides those two redeeming qualities, I never viewed him as a shining example of mental fortitude. It's no secret that I'm not a sports girlie, but after watching the Netflix docuseries *Beckham*, I officially put him on my "inspiring people" list. He made the list not because of how many goals he's scored or because of his H&M underwear Super Bowl ad, but because of how he's dealt with his mental health challenges.

Mental health issues weren't talked about as openly as they are now, even twenty years ago. I don't know if I came of age at the exact time it began to be discussed or if my parents just did a good job of checking in and nurturing my mental health, but I truly hadn't grasped that the openness about publicly discussing mental health is a fairly new phenomenon until I watched his documentary. Beckham went through phases in his career where his entire country hated him, just because he'd made a mistake or a bad choice on the pitch. The public didn't stop at simply booing him during his games—they made up obscene songs about his wife that the whole stadium would sing. The harassment also didn't stop at his place of work. He couldn't walk down the street without someone screaming at him. If he stopped at a red light, people would angrily bang on his car. Every newspaper and magazine was full of hatred for this guy. I've experienced a small fraction of that. I know what it feels like to be hated, but I only ever saw it when I opened my phone. I was able to shut off my apps and shut it out.

But he had to deal with this all day, every day. This all happened at a time when mental health wasn't being discussed, especially when it came to men, and definitely not men in sports. Yet he found a way to talk about it and heal himself.

I've been fairly open about my struggles with anxiety and depression in the past, but I haven't really totally gone there. Not with specifics. So, now seems like a good time for a trigger warning. Consider yourself warned (but stay with me). . . .

For about eleven years off and on, I had a cutting problem. I self-mutilated in order to cope with any extreme feeling of sadness, anxiety, or anger. There have been times in my life where I considered driving my car into a building, or jumping out of the window of my high-rise apartment. I know what it feels like to not want to live. I know this is a long way from the good old *Next Level Basic* days of self-care Sunday and Frappuccino Stassi, so let me start from the beginning.

At eighteen, I was a freshman at Louisiana State University. I knew I wanted to go to school in Los Angeles, but I went to LSU because I had gotten a scholarship. One night in September 2006, I got a call from a friend telling me that someone who I considered to be my mentor had committed suicide. His name is not Luke, but for the sake of his family's privacy, let's call him Luke. In my previous books I've written about how I went to a performing arts school in addition to my high school. Luke was my teacher there. He got to know my parents and my family, and started coaching me in his acting classes. We're lucky if we get one or two teachers or mentors in life who give us confidence and push us when we're younger. Luke took me seriously when I told him about my plans to go to school in Los Angeles or maybe New York. We talked about me applying to a conservatory. I was going to study, work hard, practice, and dedicate my life to becoming a great actor, and he was going to coach me through it. I read about Marilyn Monroe having these acting coaches who became her personal mentors, people like Paula Strasberg or Natasha Lytess. To me, Luke was my Natasha. He was the best, the most inspiring, the kindest. My parents were obligated to tell me I was the smartest or most talented human on earth, but here was a person who took me under his wing by choice. I'll never forget that. Someone told me that in the note he left he mentioned that he couldn't handle what had happened to New Orleans after Hurricane Katrina. There was more to it than that, but he loved the city, and seeing parts of it destroyed may have triggered something in him. Whatever it was, it was tragic. I carried his photo around in my wallet for years.

When Luke died, most of those big dreams for myself did too. At that point I was lucky enough to have never experienced loss before. I hadn't known anyone who had passed away, much less someone who took their own life. I couldn't comprehend the sadness he must have felt. His death consumed me. It was all I thought about. I stopped going to my classes and locked myself in my campus apartment and cried, all day and night. Like a true fucking masochist, I listened to "Colorblind" by the Counting Crows about a hundred times a day. It was in the movie *Cruel Intentions* and quite possibly one of the most depressing songs ever, IMO. It's a song about feeling emotionally isolated, hopeless, detached from anything remotely joyful. Talk about leaning in to one's depression. I must have really wanted to stay on theme. One day I did leave my apartment to drive to Barnes & Noble so I could buy a book on how to connect with the dead. There was a chapter on communicating with the dead in your dreams. I followed the instructions, wrote Luke a letter, put it under my pillow with some herb next to it that was supposed to help you communicate with the dead, and I went to sleep.

I swear, that night I dreamed I was in a diner and a phone rang. The waitress called me over and said it was for me, and on the other end of the line was Luke. I don't remember what he said, but it put me at ease.

I didn't know how to process anything I was thinking or feeling, but I oddly didn't want it to go away because that meant I was forgetting him.

There was another night when my roommate was sleeping at her boyfriend's place and I was in the fetal position sobbing in our kitchen. I couldn't stop crying. At that moment something came over me, and I reached for a kitchen knife. I don't know where the impulse came from. That night was the first time I cut myself. It was just a little bit on my forearm, and it calmed my hysterical sobbing. I don't know if it was the transference of emotional pain to physical pain or whether the fact that I was cutting myself just scared the shit out of me so much that it shifted my focus away from the sadness. Whatever it was, it calmed me down. I didn't do it with the intention of killing myself. The intention was to stop the sadness. After that it became a destructive, secret habit that I would rely on whenever I was going through something. Eventually I started to heal from Luke's death, but not before I started failing my classes. I knew I needed to get out of Louisiana. The thought of pursuing an acting career made me sick, but I still wanted to move to Los Angeles. I wanted to do more and experience more than what I thought Louisiana had to offer.

Because I had done so poorly at LSU, I had to do a year of community college in Los Angeles in order to get my grades back up and transfer to Loyola Marymount. While I was happy to finally be at Loyola Marymount, my mental health was a wreck. There, I was introduced to Adderall by a friend. I honestly knew more students who took it than students who didn't. We were all just trying to stay up late, write papers and study, and Adderall made all of that so much easier. The problem was that I became truly dependent on it. I didn't go a day without it. It honestly felt like it was some vitamin that was just a necessary part of my life. I convinced myself that I couldn't even answer a phone call or vacuum my apartment unless I had taken Adderall. I also drank on Adderall. I spent the next ten years consistently taking it, and during that time I went through so many periods where I would feel such extreme lows. I always turned to cutting. I laugh about the Dark Passenger now, but her origin is actually sad.

I would be sure to cut myself in places I thought were hidden. I have scars all over my hips and upper thighs, and one particularly large scar on my right ankle from when I was hospitalized. Yes, you read that correctly. I cut myself so deep that my boyfriend at the time had to take me to the hospital. That was probably my first true experience with humiliation and shame. I don't even think there's a word that can describe how it feels to look nurses and doctors in the eyes and admit that you did that to yourself. After that experience, I admitted it to my parents and did everything to try to control it. They weren't angry, they just jumped to action to help me. At this point I hadn't considered that Adderall could be fueling this. I'm very fortunate to have parents who have always prioritized my mental health. My first memory of being in therapy is age five, when my parents got divorced. They always took my feelings and moods seriously, and I always felt that my feelings were valid. I never felt as if I had to just buck up and get on with it. They always listened and tried to help.

I remember one specific night when I had tried everything to not cut myself. I chopped off all of my hair instead and ripped down my curtains and the curtain rods from the walls. I called my dad sobbing, and he flew out and took me to some specialist who was using new technology to monitor the brain in patients dealing with mental health problems. At these appointments they would place wires all around my scalp, and I would sit and listen to weird sounds. After a handful of sessions, somehow, based on which areas of my brain were lighting up during the session, they were able to tell me that I didn't suffer from depression. I suffered from anxiety. My dad got me a life coach in addition to a therapist. I tried different medications. I went through long stretches where I felt fine. But every now and then, I'd experience something that seemed too painful, and the cutting would creep back in. It always felt like a dirty secret.

It wasn't until I met Beau that I was able to stop cutting and quit Adderall. In October 2018, a big group of us went to Cabo San Lucas, Mexico, for Lala's birthday. I took Adderall first thing in the morning and proceeded to drink the whole day and night. I had Bloody Marys on the plane and margaritas when I got there, with tequila shots thrown in between, which probably didn't help alleviate any dark thoughts I was having. My memory of the string of events afterward is hazy. What I do remember is going absolutely crazy inside our room while Beau was gone. It was like one of those exorcism movies, where the priest visits the house of someone who is seemingly possessed, and the possessed person is incoherent and violently throwing themselves around the room. That might sound like I'm making light of the situation, but I'm not. I was completely out of control.

I rage-texted and called Beau over and over on repeat, because I was angry he had gone to dinner instead of staying back with me. I'm talking almost a hundred crazy texts and nonstop calling back-to-back. I was feral. And then I remember cutting the side of my hip. Now this is where I am the most ashamed. This is the part that's the hardest to write and admit. It's maybe one of the most vile, manipulative, horrible things I've ever done, and it's the scariest thing to put out there in the world, but I'm going to admit to it. At this point I sent both Beau and Katie Maloney photos of what I had done to myself. If that's not one of the most twisted and cruel things to do to someone, I don't know what is. I'll live with that guilt forever. Beau left the dinner and came back, and I remember him telling me that he needed to call his mom and be away from me to think. I may have mentioned something about the cutting to Beau, but I had never sat him down to say, "I have a problem." I eventually fell asleep, and he spent the majority of the night elsewhere on the phone with his mom. We woke up the next morning, and he said if that ever happened again, even in the slightest bit, he'd be out of the relationship. It was the wake-up call I needed. I had finally found the person I wanted to spend my life with. He was trustworthy; he was loyal; he was supportive; he was moral. I wasn't going to lose him. So that day I quit Adderall. And that was the last time I ever hurt myself. Beau saved me that day.

The thought of cutting myself hasn't crept into my mind once since that night. I've had some pretty dark days since then (hello, postpartum lows), but I've never been tempted. Maybe the thought of losing my relationship scared the shit out of me so much that it cured me. I also know that I could never be tempted to hurt myself, because of my children. They've given me so much purpose, and so much to live for (even when they have epic meltdowns). I need to be the best version of myself for them. I meant it when I wrote that Hartford saved me in *Off with My Head*. If I hadn't been pregnant when I was canceled, maybe those thoughts of self-harm would've come flooding back. I was strong because of her. Beau and my children have saved me when my life could've gone in a very dark direction.

I know I was lucky to get through that, and there are so many people who struggle. Even though people have become so much more open about mental health (Chrissy Teigen, Demi Lovato,

Prince Harry, Justin Bieber, Miley Cyrus), I don't really talk about it with other mom friends, and not even with my unicorn mom friend. Then again, no one is going to randomly bring up depression or anxiety at the neighborhood park or casually mention it while you wait for your kids outside a Halloween bounce house. When you go out with friends for a fun night, who wants to bring down the vibe unless it's a serious situation? Those are times to take off the pressure, not pile it on. Still, I know how important it is to sometimes not sweep things under the rug. I wasn't ready to talk about these things before, but now I know how important it can be.

I still have my moments, but I never think of harming myself. It can still be scary though. After Messer was born we got home from the hospital on a Friday, and that Sunday I was full-on possessed by a demon/Dark Passenger Stassi. I had not felt that low, that sad and terrified, in years, if ever. Looking back now, I can see that it was probably hormones, but I felt so awful that I was having uncontrollable dark thoughts and sobbing and yelling at Beau. He told me to go into the bedroom and try to calm down, not to be condescending, but to try and calm the house down a little bit. I could not stop crying, and I wound up so swollen and blotchy I looked like I'd just spent fifteen rounds inside of a UFC ring with some fighter dude in tiny clothes. Suddenly during all of this crying I had a powerful urge to get the baby back, so I ran upstairs and screamed at Beau, "Give me my baby!" I'm sure he was terrified. I texted my doctor and explained how I was feeling (horrible) and acting (also horrible), and he told me that this was "very normal."

EXCUSE ME? Very normal? Like, other women experience this level of rage, anxiety, and terror after birth too? It did not feel normal to me at all.

Eventually my mood settled, and thankfully it lasted for only that day, but it was scary. Obviously I have days where I feel down or anxious, but nothing like that. There is no girlbossing when it comes to mental health. I mean, you can work out every day and eat only healthy foods and go to sleep at 9 p.m. (if that sounds good to you) for your physical health, but when it comes to actual brain chemistry and anxiety, it's harder to know what steps to take that will actually help. No one is "the best" at mental health. Even the most Zen girlies probably have their moments. Look at Barbie. Yes, she's a fictional character in a movie that's based on a doll, but she had anxiety too. It's part of being human (or a doll I guess). You just have to try different approaches and ask for help when you need it.

My kids lift me up, but as anyone with toddlers probably knows, they can also knock you the *eff* down. When we were on our 2023 podcast tour, we flew back home from Boston on Mother's Day. I was pregnant, and it was the longest leg of our tour, so I missed Hartford like crazy. The hotel we stayed in even decorated the room with photos of me and Hartford, which was so sweet, but it made me want to get back to my baby so badly. When we finally got home, I saw my little girl and held my arms open for a hug, and she completely ignored me and yelled, "Papa! Papa!" She did not care at all, and it was Mother's Day! Beau eventually left to get some groceries and while he was gone, Hartford spent the time having a code red meltdown, hitting me and the dogs and acting like Damien from *The Omen* mixed with a velociraptor. I tried to reprimand her, first by calmly saying things like "We don't hit," and then by pleading with her, and finally by raising my voice a little. I guess Hartford won the battle of wills, because I ended up sitting on our staircase in tears.

When Beau came back home, I was crying so hard, with Hartford sitting right next to me, that he thought I was joking. Not only did I not get a simple (and much needed) hug on Mother's Day, I was panicking that we had a physically violent toddler on our hands who might turn into a physically violent adult one day. Eventually I stopped crying and she stopped tormenting me, and I realized that most toddlers just love to antagonize a parent and it doesn't mean they'll grow up to be murderers. Still, kids are experts at pushing buttons and knowing just how to set us off sometimes. I got my Mother's Day snuggles in the end, but she put me through hell to get there! The one thing that brings me the most joy in life (my kids) is also the thing that can push me toward a nervous breakdown. Good times! I do worry about Hartford, since she has big feelings too. I know that's typical for toddlers, but I'm just careful to treat her the way I'd want to be treated when I'm melting down. I want her to have a healthy experience with emotions, so I worry about her mental health, and try to treat her with respect EVEN when she's acting like a toddler version of Godzilla.

So the days of self-care Sunday may be over, but I still put on my makeup and jewelry when I need a pick-me-up, and I still put serums on my skin because it relaxes me and helps even out my moods. I still don't love to work out, but I do this EMS (electro muscle stimulation) workout at home that takes only about twenty minutes. It looks ridiculous because you put on this black bodysuit thing with wires attached to a machine, but I swear it works. It feels like you're getting mildly electrocuted while you do squats, but really the machine is just helping your muscles contract more, enhancing the workout. It helps my mood because I feel like I'm doing something physically good for my body, which then helps my mind. I also light candles every single morning. I don't know why, but it makes me feel good. I can't get the kids up until I light a candle. I put on a YouTube channel with Victorian Christmas sounds, like a snowy cobblestone street with carriages and little shop bells. That's all helpful, but you know what else is helpful? Getting away, by myself, for twenty-four to forty-eight hours. A few months after Messer was born I went to Philadelphia for a quick work trip. I felt so guilty at first, leaving Beau and the kids, but my guilt melted as soon as I walked into the hotel room, put on a robe, and poured a glass of wine. I watched Netflix, I relaxed, I spied on the people in the high-rise building across the way from me. Before you freak out about boundaries, it was an office building, so the most fascinating thing I saw was someone vacuuming the floor. Still, it was the best. I didn't need a spa vacation or a villa in Tuscany to lift my mood. I just needed a robe, a hotel, some mild spying, a glass of wine, and the ability to let it all go.

Honestly, I'm still scared about opening up on the page like this, even in my own book. It's hard to share things like this, and I'm terrified that these are the things that will be pulled out as headlines, little snippets without any context, so that people click. It's worth it to say these things though. It's my hope that it makes you feel less alone if you've ever struggled with it, and know that if you've ever envied another person, they might be dealing with something like this behind the scenes. It's that whole switching-lives philosophy again—you have to want every part of someone else's life to be them.

Takeaway

Self-care is about so much more than colonics or vampire facials. It's about being honest about how you're feeling and what you need, getting real help when things are tough, and giving yourself permission to say ENOUGH. Don't stress if you're not doing a nightly mud mask or meditating every morning. Just do what you need to do to feel okay; and I swear, Victorian ambiance YouTube is a vibe.

Badass Girlfailures

This list may seem slightly all over the place, but bear with me. I know that Taylor Swift, Anna Delvey, and Fleabag aren't normally grouped together, but hey, they've all had their low moments, just like the rest of us. And they all pulled through. Well, sort of.

✳ **KOURTNEY KARDASHIAN:** Let me first just start by saying that I love all the Kardashians and do not have a favorite. However, I do have some thoughts when it comes to the way the world views Kourtney. She's constantly lamenting about her job and family, and everyone wants to put her in this "anti-girlboss, doesn't want to work" category. She's known as the "lazy" or "failure" sister. Yet, when I look at her life, I don't see anything lazy about it. She's filmed a million seasons of *KUWTK*, she founded Poosh, she created her health brand, Lemme, and just gave birth to her fourth kid. What part of that is girlfail-y or lazy? Yeah, she complains that she doesn't want to film and that she wants to just have a quiet life on a vineyard in Italy somewhere, and live her "la dolce vita" life. But who doesn't?! Don't we all complain about our jobs every now and then? And wouldn't we all want to retire on the Amalfi Coast? Like, duh. I think she may actually be the one who has got it all figured out. She's the perfect example of someone who girlbosses a little and knows when it's time for a little breaky break.

* **MARTHA STEWART:** I mean, talk about a rebrand. Growing up, I don't ever remember thinking of Martha Stewart as cool. In fact, it was a little bit of the opposite. She had this overly buttoned-up, stuffy, homemaking image. Nothing about it was aspirational or even likable to me. And then she SERIOUSLY girlfailed. Like "went to freaking prison" girlfailed. "Doesn't get any worse than that" girlfailed. I couldn't believe it at the time. The absolute last person I ever thought I would see in prison was in prison. Granted, it was a cushy prison and not Rikers Island, but still. The second she got out, she revamped her image and launched her comeback. She was a homemaker with an edge. She's kind of everything I want to be now. I mean, have you seen her thirst traps? Stunning, gorgeous. I even bought the replica of her Christmas nativity she made when she was in prison. Yes, she found a way to build a Christmas nativity in prison.

* **ELIZABETH HOLMES:** Before you come at me, I am *not* defending Elizabeth Holmes. But I bet she wishes like hell she would've embraced the middle ground instead of squeezing into those black turtlenecks day after day in her quest to be an ultimate girlboss. I mean, imagine if she was just like, "You know, I'm smart, I know business and tech, but I don't need to be INFAMOUS." She might be anony-

mously relaxing in Menlo Park right now, not having it all, but also not having a jail sentence.

✳ **CARRIE BRADSHAW:** In my early twenties, I worshipped Carrie Bradshaw. Now, in my thirties, I'm repulsed by her. Sure, she looks like she's girlbossing on the outside, but IMO, she's a total girlfailure. Like, sure, she lives a glamorous life and professionally she's killed it, but . . . she kind of sucks. Like, really sucks actually. As a human being, she may be the worst. She's selfish, she's a bad friend, she cheats on her boyfriends, she is never not acting like the victim, and after the lifelong roller coaster that was her relationship with Mr. Big, after he died, like for real DROPPED DEAD, she actually said, out loud, "Was Mr. Big a big mistake?" CARRIE, PLEASE STOP TALKING. For obvious reasons I'm not a huge fan of cancel culture, but please can we all agree to cancel Carrie Bradshaw?!

✳ **SERENA VAN DER WOODSEN:** See Carrie Bradshaw. Same shit, just the younger millennial version.

✳ **ANNA SOROKIN AKA ANNA DELVEY:** Another one who didn't let a little thing like prison get her down. After serving time in prison she was supposed to be deported back to Germany, but somehow she managed to finagle a way to stay confined in her $4,250-a-month NYC apartment with electronic monitoring, where she restarted her girlbossing ways and started making and selling art. Neither prison nor house arrest nor any girlfailing can keep her from girl-bossin'.

✳ **TAYLOR SWIFT:** I can't recall ever feeling like Taylor Swift was canceled, but after reading her *Time* interview and watching *Miss Americana*, it's very clear that she felt canceled and had a major girlfailure moment. And. Look. At. Her. Now. The most successful female of the last year?! I wonder if she would've gotten here had she not gone through her girlfailure moment. Not only did it provide inspiration and subject matter for new songs, but also maybe it motivated her to do things she had never done before and to break pretty much every record she could. And on top of all that, part of what we love the most about her is how she embraces her flaws. She takes her girlfail-ures, uses them as themes for her music, and turns them into successes. To call her a girlboss wouldn't do her justice. It's almost rude. We need a new word for her level.

✳ **LORELAI GILMORE:** As I've mentioned already, I spent my postpartum weeks watching *Gilmore Girls* for the first time, and I've come to realize that while I do love Lorelai, she thrives only when she's failing. If things in her life are going a little smoothly, she's gotta go fuck it all up some-how. And when her parents want to help her out of any tough situation, she refuses and acts like they're awful human beings who just want to control her. Girl, maybe they just want to help their daughter out. Maybe it's not that deep?! We all have that one friend who thrives in chaos but is always like, "Why does drama follow me??!" Like, girl. You *are* the drama.

﹡ **MEGHAN MARKLE:** So many of you are out here calling my girl a failure on the reg, and I'm gonna need it to stop now. This is another Kourtney Kardashian situation, where I think a lot of people have got it seriously twisted. Has Meghan Markle failed at some things in her life? Yes. Is she a failure as a person? Fuck no. So what if her podcast didn't do well and got canceled, not every little thing we try and do is always going to be a success. To all the keyboard trolls out there who love to hate on Meghan and attack her for her failures, have you never failed at anything in your life? Have you succeeded in every little thing you've attempted? Meghan's girlfailures make me respect her more, because she never lets it deter her. Also, it's relatable as shit to know that she doesn't win at everything. I'd say her life with her husband and two children and their enormous Montecito mansion is maybe the opposite of being a hot mess. If that's girlfailing, I want to girlfail too.

﹡ **OLSEN TWINS:** This one is a little more nuanced. First of all, the Olsen twins are my everything. I grew up with them (not in real life, just their movies, duh). They influenced so much of my adolescence. *Passport to Paris*; *Holiday in the Sun*; *Our Lips Are Sealed*; *Double, Double, Toil and Trouble*?! The list goes on. I wanted to dress like them, wear my hair like them, breathe like them. And then in peak Olsen-mania, they decide to close it up and start a luxury clothing line. Of course the fashion industry laughed at this idea. Two twin teenage actresses attempting to become serious fashion designers? They had to deal with those girl-failures of not being taken seriously in their new profession. But now, almost twenty years later, the Row is one of the most respected clothing brands out there. Despite the huge possibility of failure, they completely switched careers and never looked back.

✳ **ELLE WOODS:** She is the actual definition of someone who is at the intersection of girlboss and girlfailure. Supposedly she's this bimbo whom no one takes seriously, and yet she manages to not only get into Harvard Law School but also graduates valedictorian and wins a murder case?! If she had been around IRL in the age of TikTok, she would've 100 percent gone viral and become the first ever lawyer/fashion hybrid influencer. Sure, she had lots of failures along the way, but I think most girlbosses would say that girlfailing comes with the job every now and then.

✳ **FLEABAG:** The ultimate representation of what it means to not just fail at things but to be considered a screwup as a human being by everyone around her. Yet we still all wanted to root for her? What does that say about us as a society? I think that we all have a bit of girlfailure in us and we just want to relate and feel like someone else is failing a little bit more than we are. Fleabag fully delivered us an example of someone who couldn't be fucking up life more, but we loved her for it.

✳ **KESHA:** I personally believe that when one finds themselves in a position where they write a lyric about brushing their teeth with a bottle of Jack, it may be time to reconsider some life choices. Obvs no judgment though. Kesha literally built her brand off of being the hot-mess, party-animal pop star. But today? I literally weep whenever I listen to her song "Praying." She turned the pain that she endured into some of the most powerful music I've ever heard. And her song "Woman"? Ultimate girlboss vibe song.

✳ **ANYONE WHO HAS EVER CAPITALIZED ON BEING A HOT MESS:** So, basically any reality star to ever exist. Essentially . . . me. Yep, I'm adding myself to this list. We reality folk take our girlfailures, our flaws, our weaknesses, our imperfections, our blemishes, our faults and we put it all out there so viewers can relate or feel less alone. Maybe we do it to give viewers a laugh and a break from the stresses of everyday life. We become the butt of the joke. Sometimes we're in on it, sometimes we're not. We get people picking apart our every move and word. But sometimes we manage to take sour-ass moldy lemons and turn them into limoncino. For example, this book, and my last book, and the one before it. I'm no stranger to girlfailure. In fact, sometimes I feel like I experience girlfailure just as much as

I experience girlsuccess. But one thing I know about failure, and the low moments, the challenges, the days you want to scream or the nights you are so exhausted even your eyelashes hurt . . . those moments all lead to the same thing, if you just remember to take it easy on yourself and take the pressure off. It always, *always*, leads to new beginnings.

CHAPTER 13

What Kind of Bonne Bell Lip Gloss Are You?

The 2023 holidays were my first winter holidays as a mom of two. They were also the holidays that were the least fun and most stressful of my life. There's no school, no babysitter, no nanny. I was trying to enjoy the decorations and the food and the presents, but that's not easy when your kid is tantruming 24-7 and there is sugar everywhere, which amps up the tantruming by seventeen million. One day during this joyous celebration/hell fest, I started questioning my existence and my life choices. I looked at Beau and said, "We chose this."

He understood. I just could not watch Blippi or Ms. Rachel on YouTube *one more time*. I needed to watch something dark and relatable. Something like *A Bad Moms Christmas*.

I had seen this movie multiple times before, but on that day, it hit so hard. The three main characters are moms (played by Mila Kunis, Kristen Bell, and Kathryn Hahn) who lean way into their hot-mess sides and rebel against Christmas by doing crazy shit and defying the "good mom" stereotype. They give total girlfailure vibes, which made me love and need them in that moment. There's a scene where they're shopping at the mall for Christmas gifts and they see all these parents dragging around screaming kids, and the bad moms are like, "If we're going to do this, we need to drink." So they drink beers at the mall food court and get messy, which was so comforting! I love that fuck-it mentality. It was exactly what I needed at that moment. I was like, I may be struggling to enjoy this holiday as a mom and failing at girlbossing my way through it, but look at these moms! I know they're not real people, but still. I posted some cute photos of me and Beau at Christmas brunch with the kids during that time, but I warned people not to be fooled. We sat in silence during that brunch, just shells of our former selves because of the 8,700 tantrums raging between each photo. I did not feel like I had it all together. And you know what, I have come to accept that that is okay.

I started out to write this book not just for you but for me. I am not an expert at "having it all" or "girlbossing" or being a badass mom/wife/daughter/friend/businesswoman/human. Part of the struggle is we are so pressured to define ourselves or fit a certain box or type: Are you a chill mom or a helicopter mom? A strawberry girl or a tomato girl? Maybe cottagecore is your thing, or is it dark academia? A girlboss or a girlfailure? Why is there so much push to define ourselves? It's exhausting.

WHAT TYPE OF TIRED MOM ARE YOU? 🌙 zzz

RUN-DOWN	WEARY	WORN-OUT
MUTANT MOM WHO'S NOT TIRED BUT PEPPY	TRULY EXHAUSTED	BONE-TIRED

I have a theory. I think it started with the quizzes.

There was a time when every teen magazine had personality quizzes like "Which Bonne Bell Lip Gloss Flavor Are You?" or "Which Spice Girl Are You?" They weren't exactly *scientific*, but we all did them. We all wanted to know which boy band member was our perfect match or what OPI nail polish color best represented our personality and why. Those quizzes then evolved into the more "adult" *BuzzFeed* quizzes like "Uncover Your Witch Persona by Selecting Your Favorite Morning Meal."

For real. I decided to dive into some serious research for this chapter, so I found a "What Restaurant Chain Are You?" quiz. I got

Chili's because I have zest and spunk. I mean, not after taking care of two kids all day, but nice try. There are now a million ways we can categorize ourselves thanks to TikTok, but the two that seem to creep in a lot are the girlboss and the girlfailure. The thing is, we don't have to be either, or we can be both at once, or alternate between the two during any given day. When trying to be a boss gets overwhelming, though, we lean into the hot messes. Like the Bad Moms, their messiness gives us hope.

Obviously there will be low moments when we feel like we are not winning at life or work or relationships and that's human. I took a hiatus during seasons three and four of *Vanderpump*, mainly because my asshole ex-boyfriend Manbun didn't like reality TV. During that time I gained a bunch of weight and moved into my mom's place. I was living out of a suitcase, and we were drinking protein shakes mixed with vodka (we were trying to lose weight but *also* enjoy the process). It felt like my life had gone up in flames, and we would just watch romantic comedies and talk about the fact that our lives were such shitshows. That time made me appreciate what I had with the show, and it made me miss my friends. I missed working. So I talked to the producers, and after they made me grovel and squirm a little bit (their standard MO), I returned to *Vanderpump* with a new determination to not live out of a suitcase and not have vodka protein shots for lunch. When I went back, one of the first things I said on camera was, "When you don't have your shit together, you have to dress like you do." I was straddling being a boss and failing even then. I turned that sentiment into my own national holiday, National #OOTD Day. You know you are in full girlboss mode when you take the time to create your own holiday.

When it comes to girlbossing or girlfailing, having it all (or so I thought) and being at rock bottom, I feel like most of my adult life has been like those EKG readings where the line zig-zags up and down. Aren't we all like this though? Even Oprah and Taylor Swift have their down moments. In *Miss Americana*, the 2020 documentary about her life, Taylor Swift said she felt like she'd been canceled. To any human or alien looking at her life at that time, it would definitely not look like she was fail-ing, at least from the outside. She was *Time*'s 2023 Person of the Year, and even in that article she admitted that she didn't always feel like a boss. Far from it. Look at her song "Anti-Hero." She's telling the world that she's the problem, she screws up. She's embracing her imperfections. If the Bridget Jones books and movies came out today, the character would totally be singing those lyrics alone in her apartment while drinking straight from a bottle of chardonnay.

Bridget Jones's Diary was one of my favorite movies as a teenager. It was a comfort watch for my mom and me. I assumed that that's what I'd be like as an adult: single, unable to cook, and spending the holidays alone with wine. Like her, I'd be messy. My friends and I embraced being a hot mess, and Bridget was the first example that may have shaped the fact that we started embracing a hot-mess kind of life.

I mean, for most of *Vanderpump Rules* (okay, maybe for the whole entire time) I was messy. During my last two seasons I tried to get my shit together, but I always knew that the hot-mess part of my personality was something people liked to see, so I never fully pushed it away. I even played it up a little for the show. I did my best scene work hungover because I didn't care what came out of my mouth. Those made for the best scenes with the most drama. I didn't pretend to be someone else—I was always 100 percent myself—but I just fully leaned into drinking and drama and making mistakes.

After *Bridget Jones*, we had *Bridesmaids*. Annie's character had major Bridget Jones/girlfailure energy. So many of us relate to messy girls because they make us feel seen. They remind us that maybe you won't or can't "have it all" during every phase of your life, but that doesn't mean you can't still be a badass. I'm just done with the pressure to be one or the other. I'm trying—*trying* is the key word—to go easy on myself and remember that some days I'm a spunky Chili's restaurant, while other days I'm just a sad Wendy's with their square, disgusting hamburgers. I love scrolling through TikTok trends, and if I had to choose, I'd go full dark academia, but none of us are just one thing. I know I've long defined myself as a basic bitch, which might sound hypocritical, but my definition of a basic bitch is just someone who leans into the things that bring them joy, even if other people might make fun of them or say it's lame. So maybe I'm a basic bitch who is learning not to take myself too seriously while also raising two kids and adulting like a boss, except on the days when my adulting looks more like a fifteen-car pileup. On those days, I'll just shrug it off, take a break, and watch *Bad*

Moms or *Bridget Jones* until I stop stressing that I'm some kind of failure.

The thing about failures is that once you get over the pain or insecurity of it all, you then have the freedom to be someone different. You can shift your life, try new things, go into a different type of work or go after a different kind of partner. Once you heal, failing is good for the soul. I hate that phrase "when one door closes another door opens" because *how* and *why* does another door open? Is it by magic? What if another door doesn't open and you're just sitting there passively waiting for it to happen? That saying is bullshit. Maybe you need to get up and find your own new door and open it up. Find your escape route. Maybe it's not a door but up an air vent, like the vents that movie hostages are always crawling through. Maybe that air vent doesn't lead to where you wanted it to, but maybe it leads somewhere better. For all we know that dusty-ass air vent could lead to a Hemsworth brother or a winning lottery ticket. Basically what I'm saying is that we're gonna girlboss at times, girlfail other times; some days will be great, others you'll question the point of your own existence; many things won't pan out the way you had

intended, so you may as well give yourself permission sometimes to just say "Fuck it." Your journey may not look the way you thought it would—you may wind up dirty, tired, and slithering along an air duct instead of breezily waltzing through a magical door. That doesn't mean you're a girlfailure or any type of failure at all. It means you're a badass bitch, finding your way.

Acknowledgments

*n*ot to bring the vibe down or anything, but this book was not as easy to write as my previous two. That might come as a surprise considering the subject matter in *Off with My Head*, but it's true. I think it was the most challenging because I find the very act of writing a book to be girlbossy, which at the time contradicted everything I was writing . . . which therefore was a bit of a mindf*ck. There were so many moments where I felt at war with my thoughts. The reason I'm admitting to all this is to show even more why these acknowledgments are so important, because everyone I'm going to mention truly helped this book become what it is when I was on the verge of turning into some version of Johnny Depp's character in *Secret Window*.

Beau, don't think for a second that I take your patience for granted. I know that I tend to let stress bring me dangerously close to Dark Passengering. The way you remain so unbothered, so understanding, and so supportive of me makes me feel so loved and safe. Having you as a partner is exactly what makes it possible for me to do things like writing this book. Trust, I know how lucky I am. And I couldn't love you more.

Lo French, my COLo, the generator to my manifestor, what a journey, as always, amirite?! Besides the fact that you literally always find a way to turn any idea I have into a reality, I also wouldn't have been able to write this without our 8,327,566 brainstorming sessions. I'll never forget the first one, when this book was just an idea, and we sat around my dining table with a dry-erase board spidering out all the thoughts. You always know exactly what to say to inspire me into action.

Dina Gachman, I couldn't imagine what I would do without you on this six-year literary voyage. There were quite a few moments of panic and self-doubt, and you were the one who got me through them. You knew exactly how to put me at ease. When I got frustrated, you made it enjoyable again. I can't thank you enough for all of it.

My Gallery Books team, I adore you. Natasha Simons, you are so creative and your eccentric ideas make all of us better. (Mushroom-head fairy princess vibes next time.) You are truly one of a kind. Thank you for always hanging in there with me, despite my emotional outbursts, haha. Sally Marvin and Julia McGarry, working with you guys on the *Off with My Head* tour made me want to write another book to do it again, and here we are.

My WME crew, y'all brought me back to life. Drew Welborn, I know I've said this to you before, but I need to hammer it home. You started my career again and I will never forget that. Alyssa Reuben, I could not have dreamt up a more perfect person to not only fight for me but also handle my irrational writers-block neurosis. I love you guys.

Diandra Escamilla and Cait Bailey, your faith in me over the last few years has done so much for my self-esteem. You've made me believe in myself. And you guys make me feel like I'm still cool, so thank you.

Joe Weiner, what are we going on, fifteen years now?! You're the OG on this team. Thank you for being such a trustworthy good dude.

And finally, to the Khaleesis (IYKYK), the way y'all have given me such a profound sense of purpose. I'm fully aware I'm not curing a disease or delving into rocket science, but connecting with you guys has made me feel like I have contributed to something in a positive way. Thank you for sticking around and never ghosting me.